Cardamom & Coriander

A CELEBRATION OF INDIAN COOKING

Simon Morris

metro

This book is dedicated to
my mother and father

First published in Great Britain in 1998
by Metro Books (an imprint of Metro Publishing Limited),
19 Gerrard Street, London W1V 7LA

British Library Cataloguing in Publication Data.
A CIP record of this book is available on request
from the British Library.

Editor: Bridget Jones
Design: Roger Walker
Photography: Sian Irvine
Stylist: Joy Skipper

ISBN 1 900512 48 3

10 9 8 7 6 5 4 3 2 1

Typeset by SX Composing DTP, Rayleigh, Essex
Printed in Great Britain by CPD Group, Wales

Contents

Acknowledgements

Very special thanks to the following.

William Henderson for endless hours of work and help.
Maggie Pearlstine, my agent, for helping me get the book off the ground.
Matthew Baylis and Toby Green at Maggie Pearlstine Associates for help and understanding.
Ida and Rollien Fernandes in Bombay for some excellent recipes and hours of teaching.
Lali Nayer, who has become a great friend, and who first introduced me to India.
Austan and Beryl Henderson, who spent hours on a computer and provided endless lunches.
All the staff at the Taj Mahal Hotels in Bombay and Hyderabad, with whom it has been a pleasure to work.
Susanne McDadd, and everyone at Metro Books.
All the families and street vendors for teaching me how to cook authentic Indian food.
My chief tasters: my mother, father, sister Nicola and brother Stephen, and finally, by no means least, Major, my black labrador, whose love of Indian food is as great as mine.

Introduction

When you pick up this book, you may wonder why a non-Asian is writing about Indian cookery. The answer is quite simple: I have a love and passion for good, exciting, authentic and well-presented Indian food. In 1997, this enthusiasm led to my becoming National Curry Chef of the Year, the first non-Asian to win the award. The competition involved winning a regional cook-off and then, as one of the 22 regional finalists, heading off to London to battle it out in the Grand Final. We were allocated 50 minutes in which to cook a main course, plain rice or chapatis and a vegetable dish. I cooked Hyderabadi Lamb with Rice and Peas (see page 82), mixed Indian vegetables and plain chapatis garnished with curry leaves. Presentation was all-important and I kept it simple, but used authentic pots which I had bought on my various visits to India. Winning the award has been the highlight of my career so far.

I started cooking at an early age with my mother, who is an excellent cook, and she has a great passion for Indian food. As a family, we used to eat out at least twice a month, often at Indian restaurants and I became addicted to Indian food. I am sure the British love affair with Indian food stems from our liking for stews and casseroles; after all, many curries are just spiced casseroles, with tender meat braised and served in an aromatic gravy.

Indian food, whether from the north or the south, is always exciting to cook and eat. Its different textures, colours and cultural background come together to produce one of the most loved cuisines in the world. From the dhals of the north to the black pepper from Cochin, the ingredients are blended with skill and care to produce dishes that become firm favourites once they are sampled.

I first experimented with Indian cooking as a hobby and soon became so hooked on it that I headed off to India on a working holiday to learn more. Since then I have travelled all over that massive country, to the north, south, east and west. I would find it difficult to say which was my favourite region, but I confess to having a soft spot for Hyderabad in Andhra Pradesh. I cooked in the Hyderabadi Club, a colonial Victorian house with large lawns and three outside kitchens serving stunning food. I was lucky to work in those kitchens and gathered some very valuable experience.

The most exciting, but dangerous, way to travel around India is on a motorbike. I love motorbikes, especially vintage ones, and in India the most famous make is the India Enfield. This famous machine, manufactured in Madras, was originally designed and built in Redditch, a town just 8 miles from my home in Bromsgrove. I always hire an Enfield when I go to Goa, but I have found Bombay roads just too dangerous, so I stay very much in the passenger seat. Although no one drives above 40 miles per hour, the rule of the road is 'first come, first served' and, as a result, motorbike accidents are all too common.

I also worked in what is probably India's most famous hotel, the Taj Mahal in Bombay. On a good day, this hotel serves up to 8,000 meals, cooked by 250 chefs. I was lucky to work on the tandoori ovens – charcoal-fired clay ovens which reach incredibly high temperatures. The Taj Mahal has a line of four, producing hundreds of tandoori meals and a large selection of wonderful breads. These are served in their famous Tandoori Restaurant which has a sophisticated atmosphere enhanced by displays by Indian dancers in the evening.

As in many countries, the best place to experience Indian food is in the home. I have met some wonderfully hospitable people on my travels; they have taken me in and given me some of the most interesting and authentic Indian meals I have ever eaten. Home cooking is very different from hotel food since Indian homes don't have ovens. Tandoori ovens are the only ones in use and they are all in the large hotels. For domestic meals, the two main types of bread, chapatis and roti, are accompanied by one meat dish, rice and a vegetable dish. This is all placed on the table and diners help themselves.

A friend of mine, Mrs Fernandes, who lives in the Juhu district of Bombay, cooks the most wonderful food. Whenever I am in Bombay I dine at her house nearly every night. She cooks dishes such as chicken masala, brinjal (aubergine) fritters and, for dessert, dhal and rice pudding. She always lets me help and I have learned a great deal in her spotlessly clean kitchen. After she has finished cooking, she cleans and polishes all the pots and hangs them proudly in order on her wall ready for the next busy day of family meals.

Street vendors are everywhere in India, serving thousands of snacks every day. They generally offer a range of only three to five dishes, from potato bondas and pakoras to fish curry, which are usually served with chapatis, rice or a light dhal – and all for 20 rupees, equivalent to about 40p in English money. Some vendors construct makeshift benches out of beer crates with a plank of wood placed across them, but it is more usual to eat standing up.

The quality of meat in India is not always good; it is often frozen and tough. This is why you hardly ever see grilled meat on the menus, apart from chicken or kebabs. However, it is a misconception that curries are cooked to mask rancid meat, with the pungent spices disguising the flavour. I have never come across rancid meat in India; tough, yes, but never off. To make up for the limited availability of refrigerators, meat is sold killed to order or lightly frozen.

When I return to England I am always sad to leave my friends and their beautiful country; I miss the colours, the general hustle and bustle, the auto-rickshaws with their noisy two-stroke engines weaving in and out of the traffic and, of course, the food. Back in Britain, there is limited time for nostalgia when I get down to work on developing recipes from the new dishes I have discovered.

My style of cooking has produced a range of recipes that are less spicy and more aromatic in flavour. I believe that you should be able to taste all the ingredients in a dish, from the meat and vegetables to the individual spices. The balance of spices is the key to good Indian food, which should not be hot enough to blow your head off. Some dishes are great when hot and spicy, but in good hotels, restaurants and friends' homes the flavours are better tuned by well-executed preparation which produces stunning results. For example, when working in the Hyderabadi Club, I found a marvellous recipe for chicken vindaloo made with fresh mustard seeds and a hint of vinegar, all perfectly balanced.

One of the advantages of Indian cooking, especially for a dinner party, is that all the work is done in advance, leaving you to sit down with your guests and enjoy the evening. However, by its very nature, Indian food is not the most visually appealing and in India food presentation can leave a lot to be desired. I prefer a more Westernized approach and like to serve food on plain white plates to show off its colours. In keeping with the current trend for uncomplicated meals, I like to serve one meat dish with two vegetable accompaniments. Modern presentation is not bound by traditional, rigid rules and it can be far more creative, with techniques for adding height to dishes by stacking ingredients. This gives depth to the presentation, enhancing the colours and making the result pleasing to the eye. Odd (threes or fives) rather than even numbers of small items or slices are easier to arrange and they usually look more interesting on plates. Remember, the possibilities are endless and it's fun to experiment.

I've been lucky to be able to test these recipes at my family's hotel, Grafton Manor at Bromsgrove, Worcestershire. The manor was originally built in 1567 and was partly rebuilt in 1710 after a fire. It was once the seat of the Earl of Shrewsbury and at one time housed the plotters involved in the Gunpowder Plot. My father moved to Grafton at the age of 12 in 1945, just after the war, when his parents opened a rest home for the elderly. In 1980, when my elder brother, twin sister and I had finished our schooling, we sat down as a family and decided to change the business, and to open the manor as a restaurant and hotel. We have nine beautifully furnished bedrooms, a 60-seat restaurant and we can cater for up to 200 people for a wedding or similar function.

The hotel also boasts $4^{1}/_{2}$ acres of lawn, a $2^{1}/_{2}$ acre lake and a large kitchen garden producing fresh vegetables, herbs and fruit for the hotel. Indian food plays a major part in our menus, from classical regional dishes to Anglo-Indian creations. Growing our own methi (fenugreek) and coriander is easy and ensures freshness in all our dishes.

I do hope you find this book interesting and inspiring, and that you find as much enjoyment in trying these recipes as I have had in researching, cooking and writing them.

Storecupboard

My storecupboard contains the herbs and spices which I believe are essential for authentic Indian food. All the following items can be found in Asian supermarkets and you will also find that most of the larger supermarkets now stock a surprisingly specialized range of exotic ingredients. It is best to buy small quantities that you will use up quickly and to replace old stocks of all herbs, seeds and powders after 6 months, to ensure that freshness and flavour are maintained.

Aniseed
These little black seeds have a strong taste. They are excellent in savoury dishes and as a digestif after meals.

Asafoetida
Also known as 'yellow powder', this pungent spice from Afghanistan and Kashmir is used in vegetable dishes. It should be used sparingly as it has a very strong flavour.

Amchoor Powder
Fawn in colour, this powder is made from unripe mangoes. It is added to chutneys to give them a sour edge.

Basmati Rice
Used for all savoury Indian rice dishes, also in rice desserts, the grains have a distinctive fragrance and delicate flavour.

Black Cardamoms
These are larger, harder and coarser than the small green variety which are most often used. The flavour is very pungent, so they

should be used in moderation.

Black or Brown Mustard Seeds
These have a surprisingly nutty flavour when cooked and they give light-coloured dishes an attractive mottled appearance.

Chillies (fresh green)
There are many varieties of green chilli, but two types are commonly available in the average supermarket: the small slim chilli that starts off green and turns red as it ripens is hotter than the larger, plump variety.

Cinnamon
This comes in sticks, bark or ground form. I tend to use the bark form for most of my dishes, since I prefer its softer flavour. Cinnamon sticks are usually used in sweet dishes.

Cloves
Commonly available in all supermarkets, these are used extensively in north Indian cookery. They have a pungent flavour.

Coconut and Desiccated Coconut
Extracting and grating coconut flesh is hard work, but well worth it. If you don't have the time then use desiccated coconut, which is equally good in savoury and sweet dishes. Pierce two of the eyes at the top of the coconut (use a corkscrew) and drain off the water from inside, then crack the nut with a hammer. Cut out the flesh and grate it on a hand grater or in a food processor, using the grating attachment.

Coconut Milk
There is a good choice of canned coconut milk available, some sweet and some without added sugar, so be careful to check the label. Alternatively, coconut milk can be prepared from creamed coconut in block form or from dehydrated coconut milk powder. You can extract milk from fresh or desiccated coconuts by soaking the grated nut in hot water but this is far more watery than the canned variety.

Coriander Seeds

These are little beige seeds with a tangy flavour with a hint of lemon. They really add freshness to Indian dishes, and, when roasted, they taste delicious.

Cumin Seeds

Another spice that is used extensively for its unique flavour. When roasted, it is surprisingly good in savoury dishes as well as sweet. To make your own ground cumin, put the seeds into a blender or coffee grinder and grind them to a powder. The spices may be roasted first, then ground for an excellent flavour.

Curry Leaves

These can be bought from most good Indian greengrocers. Always buy fresh when available, since nothing beats the flavour of fresh curry leaves. If this is not possible, buy the leaves in medium quantity and dry them yourself.

Curry Powder

I confess to being a bit of a snob when it comes to curry powder – an ingredient that real Indian chefs regard as a hasty shortcut. However, freshly made curry powder can be handy for myriad dishes, particularly if you are pressed for time. Try adding a pinch to snacks like boring beans on toast or scrambled eggs.

MAKES ABOUT 6 TABLESPOONS
PREPARATION TIME: 5 MINUTES

3 tablespoons coriander seeds
2 tablespoons cumin seeds, roasted
1 tablespoon ground turmeric
1 tablespoon whole allspice
1 tablespoon fenugreek seeds
1 tablespoon brown mustard seeds
1 tablespoon black peppercorns
1 teaspoon chilli powder

♦ Place all the ingredients in a blender and blend until you have a fine powder. The newly-blended powder gives off such an enticingly rich, spicy odour that you might be tempted to take a good sniff, but I advise you to be cautious ... for the sake of your nostrils.

Fennel Seeds

These are larger than cumin seeds and a pale pastel green colour. They give an aniseed flavour and aroma.

Fenugreek Seeds

These yellow-brown crystal-shaped seeds are the seeds from methi or fenugreek greens and they have an earthy flavour. They look rather like colourful gravel. They are an ingredient in *panch phoran*.

Dried Red Chillies

Commonly used in British cooking for pickling, these are available from most supermarkets. They are very hot and the longer they are left to infuse in a dish, the more fiery the result.

Garam Masala

This is a versatile spice which may be added to many dishes, contributing its distinctive flavour to savoury recipes. This masala will keep for up to 6 months in a cool, dark cupboard.

MAKES 225G (8OZ)
PREPARATION TIME: 10 MINUTES

85g (3oz) cumin seeds
30g (1oz) green cardamoms
30g (1oz) coriander seeds
30g (1oz) black peppercorns
30g (1oz) cloves
1 teaspoon grated nutmeg
5cm (2in) cinnamon stick

♦ Blend all the spices to a fine powder in a blender. Pass the powder through a sieve and store it in a clean airtight jar.

Garlic

This is used extensively in Indian cookery to produce rich flavours and aromas in dishes. Always follow the suggested preparation as the way in which the garlic is cut influences the flavour: the more finely chopped or crushed, the stronger the flavour. It goes without saying that the cloves of garlic should always be peeled.

Ginger

Fresh root ginger is knobbly and covered by a beige, papery skin. Look for roots that are plump and covered by fairly smooth, fine skin. The tougher the skin, the coarser the root. Fresh, thin-skinned ginger has a finer texture and it is moist when cut. This is worth buying, preparing and freezing. It can be peeled and chopped or grated. If grating ginger, put any remaining root into a freezer and remove as and when you require it. It is also easier to grate when frozen.

Ghee

This is butter which has been clarified to remove the water content and milk solids. Ghee will keep for months and it does not have to be refrigerated; however, for good hygiene it is best to store the fat in the refrigerator. It is available from supermarkets and specialist shops; notice that many types of ghee are not actually butter but a vegetable fat product. It is easy to clarify butter: heat it gently until it stops spitting and bubbling, indicating that all the water has evaporated. There should be a white residue in the bottom of the pan. Strain off the clear yellow butter fat. Strain the remaining residue through a muslin-lined sieve. True ghee has a rich buttery taste and can be bought from good Indian grocers.

Green Cardamoms

These must be fresh as they lose their flavour when old. They are very versatile and can be used in savoury or sweet dishes. You can tell that they have passed their best when the green pods become pale and lose their powerful fresh aroma.

Kewra Essence

This is used in rice puddings and sweet dishes in the same way as rosewater; it is also used in meat and savoury rice dishes and lassi. It has a distinctive flavour and aroma derived from the flowers of the screwpine tree, also known as pandanus.

Methi
The green herb grown from the fenugreek seed, this is used extensively in Indian cookery. It has an aroma and flavour all of its own. Available fresh or dried from Indian supermarkets.

Mung Beans
Also moong beans. Small, round green beans. These are most commonly known for beansprouts, which is the sprouted bean. They may be used whole in Indian cooking, or skinned and split, when they are known as mung dhal or moong dhal.

Mustard Oil
It is important to heat mustard oil to a high temperature before using it in cooking, to maximize its 'dry' flavour. Mustard oil is also very good in pickles. Available from Indian and oriental food stores, also from some healthfood shops.

Olive Oil
Widely available and popular, this is now used in Indian cookery in place of a high proportion of animal fats. Also, the Anglo-Indian influence and concern for healthy eating has brought olive oil into Indian food.

Paprika
This is a mild spice made from ground sweet peppers. It has a bright red colour and it is sometimes used to brighten up a dish.

Panch Phoran
This mixture of whole seeds is used to flavour breads. I first came across it at the Taj Mahal Hotel in Bombay. The spice mix is rolled into naans to give them a superb flavour and aroma.

MAKES 140G (5OZ)
PREPARATION TIME: 5 MINUTES

30g (1oz) black mustard seeds
30g (1oz) fennel seeds
30g (1oz) cumin seeds
30g (1oz) nigella seeds
30g (1oz) fenugreek seeds

♦ Mix all the spices and store in an airtight jar for up to 6 months.

Saffron

This is the stamen of a particular crocus flower. It is widely available and is now farmed in Europe. Saffron contributes a delicate flavour and yellow colour to dishes, especially rice.

Sambar Powder

This ground spice mixture will keep for up to 6 months if stored in an airtight jar in a cool, dark cupboard.

MAKES: ABOUT 4 TABLESPOONS
PREPARATION TIME: 10 MINUTES
COOKING TIME: 20–30 SECONDS

2 tablespoons urid dhal
2 tablespoons coriander seeds
3 dried red chillies
1 teaspoon fennel seeds
1 teaspoon cumin seeds
1 teaspoon black peppercorns
1 teaspoon brown mustard seeds

♦ Heat a heavy-based frying pan over high heat. Add the ingredients and roast for 20–30 seconds, stirring until lightly browned.
♦ Remove the pan from heat and immediately transfer the spice mixture to a blender to prevent them from becoming too brown or tasting overcooked and bitter.
♦ Blend the spices to a powder – this will take 3–5 minutes. Cool slightly before placing in an airtight jar.

Tamarind

In this country, tamarind mainly comes in the form of blocks, but it can also be bought in bean form. It has a dark brown appearance and sour flavour. To make tamarind paste, break up the block and soak the pieces in hot water to cover, then press through a sieve. Discard the seeds and fibres.

Toor Dhal

Also known as toovar dhal, these are skinned and split red beans.

Turmeric

This bright yellow spice is used to colour dishes and give them its distinct musky flavour. It can also be bought in its root form (it looks similar to ginger with bright yellow flesh), which has been dried before it can be ground.

Urid Dhal

These are skinned and split small black beans.

Vegetable Oil

This is very versatile and it has a neutral flavour. Widely used in Indian dishes and for deep frying Indian snacks.

Yellow Mustard Seeds

These are rarely used in Indian cookery, but I have a recipe in this book for Hyderabadi Chicken Vindaloo which would be lost without them.

Note: Roasting Spices

This is done in a dry pan. Use a small heavy-based pan for a small quantity of spices; heat it over high heat, then add the whole spices and cook for 20–30 seconds, until they pop slightly and are lightly browned. Take care not to overcook the spices or they will burn and taste bitter; remove them from the pan immediately so that they do not continue to brown after the pan is taken off the hob.

Soups

Kerala Tomato Soup

Soups are versatile starters, providing warmth in winter or refreshing chilled first courses in summer. Unlike the canned variety, which I think of as a great culinary tragedy, good and spicy home-made tomato soup is very difficult to beat. This recipe is a delicious blend of tomatoes with cardamoms and coriander – a great beginning for many an Indian meal.

SERVES 6
PREPARATION TIME: 35 MINUTES
COOKING TIME: ABOUT 15 MINUTES

55g (2oz) butter
225g (8oz) onions, roughly chopped
1 green chilli, seeded and finely chopped
6 green cardamoms
1 teaspoon ground coriander
5cm (2in) fresh root ginger, peeled and roughly chopped
2 garlic cloves, roughly chopped
900g (2lb) tomatoes, quartered
1.2 litres (2 pints) Chicken Stock (see page 170)
1 teaspoon sugar
salt
1 tablespoon chopped fresh coriander leaves
10 curry leaves

◆ Melt the butter in a saucepan. Add the onions, green chilli and cardamoms, and cook for 3 minutes, stirring well.
◆ Stir in the ground coriander, ginger and garlic, then add the tomatoes and cook gently until they are soft. Pour in the stock and bring to the boil, reduce the heat and simmer for 10 minutes.
◆ Process the soup in a blender until smooth. Add the sugar and salt to taste. Reheat the soup, if necessary, before stirring in the chopped coriander leaves and curry leaves. Serve immediately.

Spicy Goan Crab Soup

The large fish market at Panjin makes Billingsgate seem dull and odourless by comparison. It is a fascinating place with varieties of fish that I had never seen before, displayed in wicker baskets. On my first visit, in the market restaurant I ordered crab soup. It was very spicy and full of flavour. I have kept the recipe in the slightly coarse and rustic form I tasted at the market, but it is also delicious blended until smooth.

SERVES 6
PREPARATION TIME: 40 MINUTES
COOKING TIME: 23 MINUTES

30g (1oz) butter
2.5cm (1in) fresh root ginger, peeled and grated
1 green chilli, seeded and finely chopped
2 garlic cloves, crushed
$^1/_2$ large onion, roughly chopped
$3^3/_4$ teaspoons coriander seeds
1 teaspoon cumin seeds
1 tablespoon paprika
$^1/_4$ teaspoon turmeric
450g (1lb) crab meat (half brown and half white)
300ml (10fl oz) coconut milk
1 teaspoon salt
1 tablespoon chopped fresh coriander leaves

♦ Melt the butter in a saucepan. Add the ginger, chilli, garlic and onion, then cook, stirring, for 3 minutes.
♦ Meanwhile, process the coriander and cumin seeds to a coarse powder in a blender. Add this to the pan with the paprika and turmeric. Stir well, then mix in the crab meat and 600ml (1 pint) water.
♦ Bring the soup to the boil, reduce the heat and simmer for 10 minutes. Pour in the coconut milk and simmer for a further 10 minutes. Stir in the salt and chopped coriander leaves, then serve immediately.

Pumpkin and Mung Bean Soup

Pumpkin makes wonderful soup; I particularly like spicing it up and creating a mix of textures by adding mung beans. This soup can be served in the pumpkin shell: slice off the top of the pumpkin and scoop out the flesh. Take care not to puncture the pumpkin shell, then reserve it and use it as a container for the soup, taking it to the table to delight your guests. Serve Tomato Chutney (see page 184) and Goan Bread Rolls (see page 162) with the soup.

SERVES 10
PREPARATION TIME: 20 MINUTES
COOKING TIME: 50–55 MINUTES

85g (3oz) mung beans
3 tablespoons vegetable oil
225g (8oz) onions, halved and sliced
2.5cm (1in) fresh root ginger, peeled and grated
2 garlic cloves, finely chopped
1 green chilli, seeded and roughly chopped
900g (2lb) pumpkin flesh, peeled and seeded
4 ripe tomatoes, roughly chopped
4 green cardamoms
1.75 litres (3 pints) Chicken Stock (see page 000)
1 teaspoon salt
1 tablespoon chopped fresh coriander leaves

♦ Half fill a small saucepan with water and bring it to the boil. Add the mung beans and cook for 8–10 minutes, or until tender. Remove from the heat and allow to cool.

♦ Heat the vegetable oil in a large saucepan and add the onions, ginger, garlic and chilli. Cook for 5 minutes or until the onions are soft, stirring occasionally. Mix in the pumpkin, tomatoes and cardamoms, then cook for a further 5 minutes.

♦ Pour in the chicken stock and bring quickly to the boil. Reduce the heat and simmer for 30 minutes, or until the pumpkin is

tender.
- ◆ Process the soup in a blender until smooth, then press it through a sieve. Add the mung beans, salt and chopped coriander leaves and reheat, stirring. Serve immediately.

Parsnip and Ginger Soup

Some of my favourite recipes combine traditional English produce with ingredients used in Indian cookery. Many classic English flavours realize their full potential when seasoned with the added zest of Indian spices and this recipe is a good example. Warming ginger complements the earthy flavour of parsnips in a soup that you will want to make time and time again as it is an all-round winner – ideal for a wintry evening fireside supper or just as presentable at an elegant dinner party. Drizzle a little mint Raita (see page 172) into the soup at the last moment to vary the flavour. Goan Bread Rolls (see page 162) are a great accompaniment.

SERVES 6
PREPARATION TIME: 40 MINUTES
COOKING TIME: 25–35 MINUTES

115g (4oz) butter
2 onions, roughly chopped
900g (2lb) parsnips, roughly chopped
10cm (4in) fresh root ginger, peeled and roughly chopped
1 tablespoon cumin seeds
300ml (10fl oz) white wine
1.75 litres (3 pints) Chicken Stock (see page 000)
salt and black pepper
chopped fresh coriander leaves to garnish

◆ Melt the butter in a heavy-based saucepan over high heat. Add the onions, cover the pan and cook gently for 3–4 minutes, or until the onions are transparent, allowing them to sweat in their own juices.

◆ Stir in the parsnips and ginger, then cover the pan and cook over low heat for 5–10 minutes. During the whole of this sweating process, do not allow the vegetables to brown.

◆ Meanwhile, fry the cumin seeds in a dry pan for 1–2 minutes, until they begin to spit and brown slightly. Transfer the seeds to a blender and process to a fine powder, then add this to the parsnip mixture.

- Pour in the white wine, stir well and cook for a further 3 minutes. Add the chicken stock and simmer the soup over medium heat for 15 minutes, until the parsnips are soft.
- Purée the soup in a clean blender and pass it through a sieve to make a very smooth soup. Reheat the soup gently and season it to taste with salt and pepper.
- To serve, pour the soup into bowls and garnish with chopped coriander leaves.

Sweetcorn, Cardamom and Coriander Soup

This was one of the luckiest mistakes I ever made when I was experimenting with sauces to complement the Chicken Terrine with Cardamom and Ginger Spinach (see page 27). I realized that what I had made was no sauce, but one of the best Indian soups I had ever eaten. The ingredients married together beautifully to produce a soup with a rich flavour and excellent texture. It is always popular and I like to serve Tomato Chutney (see page 184) as an accompaniment; allowing diners to spoon small amounts of chutney into their soup as required.

SERVES 8
PREPARATION TIME: 25 MINUTES
COOKING TIME: ABOUT 20 MINUTES

115g (4oz) butter
225g (8oz) onions, roughly chopped
4 green cardamoms
3 garlic cloves, finely chopped
2 x 340g (12oz) cans sweetcorn, drained
1.35 litres (2^1/$_4$ pints) Chicken Stock (see page 000)
^{1}/$_2$ teaspoon salt
2 tablespoons whipping cream
1 tablespoon chopped fresh coriander leaves

♦ Melt the butter in a saucepan. Add the onions, cardamoms and garlic, and cook for 3 minutes, or until the onions are softened slightly.
♦ Add the sweetcorn, stir well and cook for a further 3 minutes. Pour in the chicken stock and bring to the boil, then reduce the heat and simmer for 10 minutes.
♦ Purée the soup in a blender, then pass it through a sieve. Add the salt and reheat gently. Stir in the cream and chopped coriander, then serve immediately.

Aromatic Pea and Coriander Soup

I like using peas in my recipes because people enjoy sampling traditional English ingredients in unusual dishes. Once infused with the flavours of Indian spices, it is hard to believe that this is the same vegetable spooned out in thousands of fish and chip shops up and down the country. There is nothing mushy about this soup – when blended with ginger, onions, fresh coriander and delicate spices it makes an excellent first course. To retain the bright green colour, it is very important not to boil the soup. Remember this when reheating the soup and do so over low heat until hot, not boiling. Add the fresh coriander right at the last minute so that it retains its fresh taste.

SERVES 6
PREPARATION TIME: 25 MINUTES
COOKING TIME: ABOUT 10 MINUTES

55g (2oz) butter
225g (8oz) onions, finely chopped
3 garlic cloves, finely chopped
5cm (2in) fresh root ginger, peeled and finely chopped
$^{1}/_{2}$ teaspoon ground coriander
$^{1}/_{2}$ teaspoon ground cumin
$^{1}/_{2}$ teaspoon garam masala (see page 8)
675g (1$^{1}/_{2}$lb) frozen peas
1.4 litres (2$^{1}/_{2}$ pints) Chicken Stock (see page 170)
1 teaspoon salt
10 twists of black pepper
2 tablespoons double cream
1 tablespoon chopped fresh coriander leaves

♦ Melt the butter in a saucepan over medium heat. Add the onions, garlic and ginger. Cook for 5 minutes or until the onions are softened slightly, but not browned.
♦ Stir in the coriander, cumin and garam masala, and cook for 2

minutes. Add the peas, stir well and pour in the stock. Increase the heat and bring the stock to the boil, then immediately remove the pan from the heat.

♦ Purée the soup in a blender and pass it through a sieve. Add the salt and pepper, and reheat the soup gently without boiling. Stir in the cream and chopped coriander. Serve immediately.

Chilled Cucumber and Yogurt Soup

This refreshing soup is ideal as a starter before a barbecue on an Indian summer's day – or, for that matter, on a warm summer's day anywhere. One of the best things about this dish is that it is simplicity itself to prepare.

SERVES 4
PREPARATION TIME: 10 MINUTES, PLUS CHILLING TIME

225g (8oz) cucumber, diced
600ml (1 pint) natural yogurt
2 small garlic cloves, finely chopped
6 sprigs of mint
6 sprigs of fresh coriander
1 teaspoon paprika
1 teaspoon ground roasted cumin seeds (see page 12)
$^1/_2$ teaspoon salt

♦ Place the cucumber in a blender and add the yogurt. Add the remaining ingredients and process to a smooth creamy soup.
♦ Chill the soup for 2–4 hours or overnight.

Starters

❖

Smoked Salmon and Chick Pea Noodle Salad

This delicious and extravagant salad is ideal for a dinner-party starter, especially in summer when the cool and delicate flavours are most welcome. The salmon is carefully dressed with a variety of delicious flavours: mint raita, coriander and an exquisite clove and cardamom dressing. This exotic mélange is perfectly complemented by the texture of the chick pea noodles. When your guests have swooned over this, there is no way that the rest of your dinner party can go wrong!

SERVES 6
PREPARATION TIME: 30 MINUTES, PLUS 30 MINUTES' CHILLING

170g (6oz) smoked salmon, sliced
115g (4oz) cucumber, cut into matchstick strips
7 tablespoons chopped fresh coriander leaves
6 tablespoons Spicy Tomatoes with Brown Mustard Seeds (see page 133)
6 teaspoons Raita (see page 172)
6 teaspoons Clove and Cardamom Dressing (see page 176)
6 teaspoons Coriander Pesto (see page 173)
7 handfuls Chick Pea Noodles (see page 159)

♦ Cut the smoked salmon slices into matchstick strips and put them into a large bowl. Add the cucumber, coriander and spicy tomatoes. Chill for at least 30 minutes.
♦ Prepare six dinner plates: using a teaspoon, streak each plate with lines of mint raita in a zig-zag. Turn the plates through a third of a circle and streak with the mango and clove dressing. Finally, turn the plates through a third again and streak with coriander pesto. The result should be a lattice effect.
♦ Add the chick pea noodles to the smoked salmon and mix well. Divide the smoked salmon mixture evenly between the plates, piling it up to about 7.5–10cm (3–4in) high. Serve at once.

Chicken Terrine with Cardamom and Ginger Spinach

This terrine is a mixture of British and Indian ingredients and methods. I have never found a blender good enough to make the smooth mousse which is an essential part of this recipe, so sieving the mixture is a necessity. Achieving the right result is not difficult and it gives a marbling of the ginger, spinach and char-grilled chicken to create a perfect balance of flavours and textures. It is a time-consuming dish, but, in my opinion, well worth the effort and certain to impress the most discerning of diners.

SERVES 15
PREPARATION TIME: 2 HOURS, PLUS OVERNIGHT CHILLING
COOKING TIME: $1^{1}/_{4}$ HOURS

675g ($1^{1}/_{2}$lb) boneless chicken breasts or thighs, skinned and cut into 2.5cm (1in) cubes
2 eggs
2 teaspoons salt
600ml (1 pint) double cream
1 teaspoon ground cardamom
2 tablespoons vegetable oil
5cm (2in) fresh root ginger, peeled and cut into matchstick strips
2 teaspoons garlic, finely chopped
2 tablespoons finely chopped onion
225g (8oz) spinach
8 twists of black pepper
1 quantity Char-grilled Delhi Chicken, prepared as whole breasts
(see page 29)

◆ Process the chicken breasts or thighs to a smooth purée in a blender or food processor. Add the eggs and $1^{1}/_{2}$ teaspoons salt, and process again, until the mixture is almost liquid. Chill for 30 minutes.

- Gradually stir the cream and ground cardamom into the chilled mixture, then rub it through a fine sieve to remove all lumps. Chill again until required.
- Heat the oil in a saucepan. Add the ginger, garlic and onion, and fry, stirring occasionally, until golden brown. Add the spinach and cook briefly until it has wilted, stirring continuously. Stir in the remaining $1/2$ teaspoon salt and the pepper. Cook for 2 minutes then set the spinach mixture aside to cool.
- Combine the spinach with the chicken, mixing well until the spinach leaves are evenly marbled through the mousse. Line a 30 × 10cm (12 × 4in) terrine or loaf tin with cling film, pressing into the corners to expel any air and leaving extra film overlapping the edges of the terrine or tin. I find a sheet of kitchen paper useful for smoothing the film into the tin and excluding the air from the corners.
- Cut the char-grilled chicken into long strips. You will need about 450g (1lb), so any leftovers can be used for a salad, sandwiches or eaten as a snack – the cook's perk! Preheat the oven to 180°C/350°F/Gas 4.
- Half fill the lined terrine with the chicken and spinach mousse, pressing it well into the corners. Lay strips of the spicy chicken along the middle of the mousse: you should use about 6 strips. Then cover with the rest of the mousse and fold over the edges of the cling film, so that the terrine is totally enclosed.
- Put the lid on the terrine or cover a loaf tin closely with foil. Stand the terrine in a bain marie or deep roasting tin and pour in water to come to just below the top of the tin. Place in the oven and cook for 1 hour 10 minutes, until the mousse is set and just firm to the touch.
- Remove the terrine from the bain marie and leave it to cool completely without opening the cling film cover. Chill well for several hours or overnight.
- Uncover the terrine and carefully fold back the cling film. Cover with a board and invert both terrine or tin and board. Lift off the terrine or tin and carefully peel off the cling film.
- Use a sharp knife to cut the terrine into slices. Arrange one slice per portion for a first course. Leftover terrine can be kept in the refrigerator for up to 7 days wrapped in clean cling film and stored in an airtight or covered rigid container.

Char-grilled Delhi Chicken

This distant cousin to the British favourite, Tandoori Chicken, was the first meal I ate in India. In a suburb of Delhi, I came across 'The Chicken Shop', a food stall squeezed between a plush apartment block and a shanty town. After queuing for some time, I received a whole chicken in a plastic bag. I was astounded by the perfectly cooked, moist and exquisitely flavoured chicken that had survived the 10 minute auto-rickshaw ride back to my hotel room better than I had!

Obtaining the recipe from the chef involved manic gestures on my part and a bizarre interlude during which I helped him to catch a chicken in the muddy back yard behind the restaurant. The language barrier prevented me from making my request for a recipe entirely clear, but I was shown ingredients, including black cardamoms and fresh mint. I have experimented with the precious little information I received and this is the result.

I do not have a tandoor oven, but I use a small clay pot instead. Unglazed clay cooking pots are available from all high street kitchen shops and they give excellent results, especially when blackened with repeated use. The blacker the pot becomes, the deeper the flavour it imparts to the food. Alternatively, the skewered chicken can be cooked in a roasting tin in the oven, on a barbecue or under a hot grill. Offer an Indian Mixed Salad (see page 140), Raita (see page 172) and/or Chapatis (see page 165) with the chicken.

SERVES 4

PREPARATION TIME: 30 MINUTES, PLUS 4–6 HOURS'
MARINATING

COOKING TIME: ABOUT 10 MINUTES, PLUS 45 MINUTES'
PREHEATING

2 teaspoons paprika
3 black cardamoms
10 green cardamoms
1 tablespoon black peppercorns
10 cloves

1 cinnamon stick
2 tablespoons finely chopped onion
3 garlic cloves, finely chopped
1 small green chilli, seeded and chopped
150ml (5fl oz) plain yogurt
1 tablespoon chopped mint
30 curry leaves
1 teaspoon salt
675g (1¹/₂lb) boneless chicken breasts, skinned and cut into
2.5cm (1in) chunks

♦ Mix the paprika, black and green cardamoms, peppercorns, cloves and cinnamon stick in a blender and process to a fine powder.

♦ In a bowl or dish large enough to hold all the chicken, mix the onion, garlic and chilli with the ground dry spices. Then stir in the yogurt, chopped mint, curry leaves and salt until all the ingredients are thoroughly combined.

♦ Add the chicken to the spice mixture, turning the cubes to ensure they are all coated. Cover and marinate for 4–6 hours in the refrigerator.

♦ About 1 hour before cooking the chicken, preheat the oven to 240°C/475°F/Gas 9 or the hottest setting. Heat a covered, empty, clay pot in the oven for 45 minutes. While the pot heats, remove the chicken from the marinade and thread the pieces on metal skewers which will fit in the pot.

♦ Remove the pot from the oven and lay the skewered chicken in it. Place the uncovered pot in the oven and cook the chicken for 8–10 minutes, or until browned in places and cooked through. Serve immediately.

Pan-fried Chicken and Sweetcorn Fritters

Chicken and sweetcorn are perfect partners, and in this recipe they blend with green chilli and fresh coriander to make super fritters. The fritters are ideal for first courses, light lunches or picnics; they also go very well with Indian Mashed Potatoes (see page 120) or Baked Haricot Bean Curry (see page 158) for a main course. Offer Spicy Cucumber Yogurt (see page 174) or Indian Salsa (see page 171) with the fritters.

MAKES 8–10
PREPARATION TIME: 25 MINUTES
COOKING TIME: 6–8 MINUTES PER BATCH

450g (1lb) minced chicken
55g (2oz) drained canned or frozen sweetcorn
6 garlic cloves, finely chopped
1 onion, finely chopped
2 green chillies, seeded and finely chopped
1 teaspoon ground roasted cumin seeds
1 teaspoon turmeric
2 eggs
2 tablespoons chick pea flour (gram flour)
salt and black pepper
1 tablespoon finely chopped fresh coriander leaves
oil for deep frying

◆ Mix the chicken, sweetcorn, garlic, onion, chillies, cumin and turmeric. Add the eggs, one at a time, mixing in each one thoroughly. Then stir in the chick pea flour a tablespoonful at a time.
◆ Season the mixture with salt and black pepper, and add the chopped coriander leaves. Mix well to ensure that all the ingredients are thoroughly combined.
◆ Heat the oil for deep frying to 180°C/350°F). To check the seasoning, fry a little of the mixture for 2 minutes, or until cooked.

Drain well, cool slightly and taste for seasoning, adding extra salt if required.

♦ Once the mixture is seasoned to taste, divide it into 8–10 portions and shape them into small even-sized cakes. Deep fry the fritters for 6–8 minutes, until they are golden brown and cooked through.

♦ Drain the fritters on kitchen paper and serve two per portion.

Aromatic Beef Kofti

One evening, when staying with good friends, the Fernandes family, in Juhu, Bombay, I decided to repay their kindness by preparing a traditional Sunday Roast with all the trimmings. Sitting on a tiny stool in her spotless kitchen, I have learnt more from Ida Fernandes than from any book as she cooks wonderful dishes for a never-ending stream of family and friends.

Rollien, one of Ida's sons, took me to the butcher's shop. Meat in India is, at its best, poor – 'lamb' is invariably leathery mutton and frozen meat is far more popular than fresh. The shop turned out to be a corrugated iron cow-shed with straggly sides of meat hanging from the rafters. In consultation with Rollen, I decided that spaghetti bolognese would be more appropriate and ordered best mince. I was astonished when the butcher minced the beef using a very sharp knife.

Back in Ida's kitchen, I realised I had been a fool. Pasta, that staple of every English larder, is very rarely eaten in India; although Ida had heard of it, she thought it was disgusting and would never allow it in her kitchen. Farewell Bolognese!

I pretended that this did not present a problem and desperately thought of a solution as I emptied cupboards of equipment. The sight of some charcoal gave me the idea of grilling kofti, which was, thankfully, a rip-roaring success. Serve the kofti as a starter or main course: the recipe serves 6 as a starter or 4 as a main course. Goan Bread Rolls (see page 162) and Baked Haricot Bean Curry (see page 158) are splendid accompaniments.

MAKES 12
PREPARATION TIME: 30 MINUTES
COOKING TIME: 4–6 MINUTES

900g (2lb) lean minced beef ·
1 onion, finely chopped
2 garlic cloves, finely chopped
1 green chilli, seeded and chopped
2 teaspoons prepared English mustard
1 teaspoon garam masala (see page 8)

1 teaspoon salt
2 eggs
1 tablespoon chopped fresh coriander leaves
1 tablespoon dried methi
vegetable oil for cooking

♦ Place the minced beef in a bowl and mix in the onion, garlic and chilli. Add the mustard, garam masala, salt and eggs, and mix until all the ingredients are thoroughly bound together. Finally, mix in the coriander and methi.

♦ Divide the mixture in half, then divide each half into 6 equal portions. Shape each portion into a small burger or patty in your hands, making 12 small patties in total.

♦ Heat a little oil in a frying pan and cook the patties for 2–3 minutes on each side, until browned and cooked through. Alternatively, they may be grilled on a barbecue or under a hot grill. They can also be cooked on an oiled hot skillet or hot plate. Serve the kofti freshly cooked.

Lamb and Cashew Nut Kofti

This recipe comes from the Taj Mahal Hotel in Bombay, where it is a real favourite among the chefs.

MAKES 30
PREPARATION TIME: 40 MINUTES, PLUS 4–6 HOURS'
SOAKING
COOKING TIME: 4–6 MINUTES

225g (8oz) cashew nuts
450g (1lb) minced lamb
1 onion, finely chopped
4 garlic cloves, finely chopped
1 teaspoon ground coriander
1 teaspoon ground cumin
1 teaspoon turmeric
1 teaspoon chilli powder
3 green chillies, seeded and finely chopped
1 tablespoon chopped fresh coriander leaves
1 teaspoon salt
5cm (2in) fresh root ginger, peeled and grated
vegetable oil for cooking

◆ Soak the cashew nuts in water for 4–6 hours.
◆ Thoroughly mix the lamb, onion, garlic, ground coriander, cumin, turmeric and chilli powder.
◆ Drain the cashew nuts, place them in a food processor and process to a paste. You may have to add 1–2 tablespoons water to help the blending process.
◆ Add the lamb mixture and continue to process the ingredients until they form a smooth paste. Turn the mixture into a bowl, then mix in the chopped chilli, chopped coriander, salt and grated ginger until thoroughly combined.
◆ Shape the mixture into 30 balls and flatten into 5cm (2in) discs.
◆ Heat a little oil in a frying pan and cook the kofti for 2–3 minutes on each side, turning once. Drain on kitchen paper and serve hot or cold, as a starter or snack.

Goan Pork Pies

I first discovered Indian-style pork pies at Arambol, a hippie hot-spot on the northern tip of Goa, where I came across rows of dusty old Enfield motorbikes and lots of spaced-out, matted-haired hippies 'having a good time, man'. Strangely enough, unlike the tourist centres of Calangute or Baga, in spite of the unconventional crowd, Arambal was quite peaceful. I sampled a crude version of these pies in a run-down beach restaurant where the waiters were so laid back that it took 45 minutes for food to arrive at tables.

You will need three, four-hole Yorkshire pudding tins for baking the pies; alternatively, you can use individual flan dishes or large American muffin tins, but smaller patty tins are too small. Disposable individual foil pie dishes (available from supermarkets) can also be used. The pies are ideal for picnics or buffets. If you like to eat them hot, then deep fry them for a couple of minutes, until they turn an attractive mahogany brown and the filling remains moist. Alternatively, heat them through slowly in the oven. Cooled pies can be frozen for about a month: place in sealed freezer bags and thaw and reheat thoroughly before serving.

MAKES 12
PREPARATION TIME: 45 MINUTES
COOKING TIME: 1^1/2 HOURS

280g (10oz) minced pork (preferably belly pork)
115g (4oz) salami, finely diced
5 garlic cloves, finely chopped
1 onion, finely chopped
2.5cm (1in) fresh root ginger, peeled and grated
115g (4oz) dessert apple, peeled, cored and diced
5 green cardamoms
1 teaspoon coriander seeds
^{1}/2 teaspoon cumin seeds
^{1}/2 teaspoon black pepper
4 pieces cinnamon bark

2 green chillies, seeded and finely chopped
1 teaspoon salt
2 eggs

Hot Water Crust Pastry
450g (1lb) plain flour
170g (6oz) lard
$^{1}/_{2}$ teaspoon ground fennel seeds
1 teaspoon salt
2 eggs, beaten, to glaze

♦ Mix the pork with the salami, garlic, onion, ginger and apple.

♦ Heat a small frying pan over high heat. Add the cardamoms, coriander, cumin, black pepper and cinnamon bark, and roast these spices, shaking the pan occasionally, for 30 seconds. Cool for a few seconds, then grind to a powder in a blender.

♦ Add the ground roasted spices, chillies, salt and eggs to the pork, and thoroughly mix all the ingredients until they are well bound together.

♦ Make the hot water crust pastry: sift the flour into a bowl and pour 300ml (10fl oz) water into a fairly large saucepan. Add the lard and ground fennel, and heat until the lard has melted, then bring the liquid to the boil. Add the flour and salt, stirring well to make a ball of soft dough. Remove from the heat immediately and allow to cool for 5–8 minutes.

♦ Roll the pastry into a ball and cut off about two-thirds of the pastry for the pie bases. Keep the remaining pastry covered with cling film while you are not working with it to prevent it from drying out. Flatten the pastry on a lightly floured work surface and roll it out to 3mm ($^{1}/_{8}$in) thick. Dust the surface and rolling pin with a little flour occasionally to prevent the pastry from sticking to it.

♦ Use a 10cm (4in) round cutter to cut out 12 circles and use these to line Yorkshire pudding tins. Fill the pastry cases with the pork mixture, leaving a narrow rim of pastry around the edge. Brush the pastry edge with beaten egg.

♦ Roll out the trimmings with the remaining pastry and use a 6cm ($2^{1}/_{2}$in) round cutter to cut out 12 lids. Place these on top of the pork mixture and pinch the edges together to seal in the filling. Crimp or pinch the pie rims with a knife or your fingers and make a small hole in the pastry lid to allow steam to escape. Brush with beaten egg.

♦ Bake for 20 minutes at 225°C/425°F/Gas 7, then reduce the oven temperature to 160°C/325°F/Gas 3 and cook for a further 45–60 minutes, or until the pies are deep golden brown.

♦ Leave the pies to cool in the tins for 25 minutes, then transfer them to a wire rack to cool. Alternatively, to serve the pies hot, allow them to stand in the trays as this gives the pastry time to set, then transfer them directly to plates.

Indian-style Scrambled Eggs

One noisy Bombay morning, I decided that a good hot breakfast might relieve a pounding headache, the result of too much Kingfisher beer and the ugly honking from auto-rickshaw horns. I rang room service and tucked in as soon as my scrambled eggs arrived, but the first mouthful of very sweet egg made me realize that the chef must have confused the sugar with the salt.

PREPARATION TIME: 20 MINUTES
COOKING TIME: ABOUT 7 MINUTES
SERVES 4

1 tablespoon vegetable oil
30g (1oz) butter
1 tablespoon finely chopped onion
1 teaspoon finely chopped green chilli
$1/4$ teaspoon paprika
$1/4$ teaspoon ground coriander
$1/4$ teaspoon turmeric
1 teaspoon grated fresh root ginger
4 eggs
120ml (4fl oz) milk
pinch of sugar
pinch of salt
6 twists of black pepper
$1/2$ teaspoon chopped fresh coriander leaves
5 cherry tomatoes, halved

- Heat the oil and butter in a saucepan. Add the onion and chilli, and fry for 3 minutes, or until the onion browns slightly. Reduce the heat to low. Stir in the paprika, ground coriander, turmeric and ginger, then cook for 2 minutes.
- Meanwhile, beat the eggs with the milk, sugar, salt and pepper. Pour this mixture into the saucepan and cook slowly, stirring occasionally, until the eggs are just set.
- Add the chopped coriander and tomatoes. Serve immediately.

Hyderabadi Eggs

In contrast to the culture shock western visitors experience on the streets of India, the kitchens in the country's big hotels seem just like those anywhere else in the world. This similarity provides a bond between chefs and when I worked in Indian hotels I always looked forward to getting down to the business of cooking in the kitchens.

When I worked at the Taj Gateway Hotel in Hyderabad, I always started the day with some of the sumptuous buffet breakfast which offered all the Indian delicacies. When I saw them, I could not resist the boiled eggs surrounded by a spicy tomato sauce. It is a traditional dish from Hyderabad, and one of my favourites. The combination of curry spices and eggs does not have universal appeal, but this delicious dish lays all doubts to rest. The eggs can be served as a starter or light main course. Tomato and Coriander Rice (see page 146) is especially good with the eggs.

Serves 4

Preparation time: 40 minutes

Cooking time: 35–40 minutes

900g (2lb) tomatoes, chopped

1 tablespoon coriander seeds

4 green cardamoms

1 teaspoon brown mustard seeds

1 teaspoon cumin seeds, roasted

1 onion, finely chopped

4 garlic cloves, finely chopped

5cm (2in) fresh root ginger, peeled and grated

6 eggs

2 tablespoons tamarind paste

1 tablespoon vegetable oil

20 curry leaves

3 dried red chillies

1 teaspoon nigella seeds

1 teaspoon salt

$^{1}/_{2}$ teaspoon sugar
1 teaspoon dried methi or 1 tablespoon chopped fresh methi
1 tablespoon chopped fresh coriander leaves

♦ Place the tomatoes in a saucepan. Add the coriander seeds, cardamoms, mustard and cumin seeds, then pour in 300ml (10fl oz) water. Bring to the boil, then reduce the heat so that the sauce simmers gently.

♦ Add the onion, garlic and ginger. Cook, stirring, until the tomatoes have broken up and the mixture is the consistency of a thick sauce. This should take about 20 minutes.

♦ Meanwhile, hard boil the eggs for 8–10 minutes, depending upon their size. Drain the eggs and immediately rinse them under cold water, cracking the shells as you do so. Shell the eggs and cut them in half lengthways.

♦ Sieve the tomato sauce, pressing it through the sieve with the back of a wooden spoon. Pour the sauce back into the rinsed saucepan. Add the tamarind paste and mix well.

♦ Heat the vegetable oil in the frying pan over high heat. Add the curry leaves, dried red chillies and nigella seeds, and fry for 15–20 seconds. Pour the fried spices into the tomato sauce and stir in the salt, sugar, methi and chopped coriander.

♦ Add the eggs to the sauce and heat through gently over a medium heat for 4–6 minutes. Spoon the eggs and sauce on to four plates or one large serving dish and serve at once.

Potatoes with Fresh Curry Leaves

Bombay's two beaches, Chowpatty and Juhu, come alive in the early evening with families arriving by motorbike (a whole family may squeeze precariously on to an India Enfield bike) or motorized rickshaw. From toddlers to snow-haired matriarchs, everyone enjoys some form of entertainment – riding horses, flying kites or playing cards.

The beaches are also the best places to buy snacks. Bhel puri (a mixture of peanuts, chopped onion, dhal, tomatoes and coriander) is popular, best washed down with coconut milk straight from the shell, but bhaji is the snack most savoured in Bombay. At any time and in any part of town, you are likely to come across a dozen people either purchasing or eating bhaji, a dish of diced potatoes, onion and spices, which bears no relation to the soggy cannon-balls served as bhaji in most British restaurants.

I first experienced true bhaji at a hotel on Juhu beach, where it was served with a ring of puri, small deep-fried breads puffed up into crisp balls. This is one of my favourite recipes: serve it as starter or snack, or as a vegetable accompaniment.

SERVES 4
PREPARATION TIME: 30 MINUTES
COOKING TIME: 15–20 MINUTES

225g (8oz) potatoes, cut into 5mm ($1/4$in) dice
2 tablespoons ghee
1 teaspoon brown mustard seeds
10 curry leaves
3 tablespoons finely chopped onion
2 garlic cloves, finely chopped
1 small green chilli, seeded and chopped
2 tablespoons ground cumin
$3/4$ teaspoon salt
1 teaspoon cumin seeds, roasted (see page 12)
1 tablespoon chopped fresh coriander leaves

- Place the potatoes in a saucepan and pour in water to cover. Add a little salt and bring to the boil. Cook for 4–5 minutes, or until half cooked, not completely tender or they will break up when fried later. Drain and set aside.
- Melt the ghee in a frying pan. Add the mustard seeds and curry leaves; cook for a few seconds until these are sizzling, then add the onion, garlic and chilli. Cook gently over low heat for about 5 minutes, or until the onion is soft and lightly browned.
- Add the potatoes and ground cumin, and mix well. Fry for 5 minutes, or until the potatoes are lightly browned. Season with the salt, then add the roasted cumin seeds and chopped coriander leaves. Serve immediately.

Vegetable Pakoras

The best pakoras I ever tasted were bought in a lay-by on route from the Taj Mahal to Delhi, a journey of about 4 hours along roads which, in places, hardly warrant the description. Indian driving is fast, competitive and reckless, with the business of getting from A to B regarded as a challenge rather than a necessity. Luckily, my driver was very competent as well as talkative. He was fascinated by England, a country he had never visited, but about which he knew a great deal and I was grateful for conversation as distraction from the racing traffic.

Suddenly, we pulled into a lay-by and the driver dashed off to a man who was standing over a huge frying pan. He returned with two bags of the most wonderful pakoras, each with a little parcel containing a fierce green chilli chutney. He demonstrated how to dip the edge of a pakora carefully into the chutney and I was then fully occupied for the rest of the journey. Pakoras are ideal as a starter or snack and delicious with Mint Raita (see page 172).

MAKES 20
PREPARATION TIME: 35 MINUTES
COOKING TIME: ABOUT 20 MINUTES

225g (8oz) chick pea flour (gram flour)
$1^{1}/_{2}$ teaspoons chilli powder
1 teaspoon salt
1 teaspoon garam masala (see page 8)
1 teaspoon baking powder
1 teaspoon nigella seeds
1 tablespoon chopped fresh coriander leaves
115g (4oz) potatoes, cut into 5mm ($^{1}/_{4}$in) dice
115g (4oz) cauliflower, cut into florets
115g (4oz) spinach, thawed if frozen
115g (4oz) peas, lightly cooked if fresh or thawed if frozen
55g (2oz) aubergine (about $^{1}/_{2}$ small aubergine), cut into 5mm
($^{1}/_{4}$in) dice
vegetable oil for deep-frying

- Sift the chick pea flour into a bowl. Mix in the chilli powder, salt, garam masala, baking powder and nigella seeds. Gradually add 240ml (8fl oz) water, beating it in to make a smooth batter. Beat in the chopped coriander leaves.
- Cook the potatoes in boiling salted water for about 10 minutes, or until tender. Add the cauliflower to the potatoes after 5 minutes, so that the florets are lightly cooked, with a slight crunch.
- Place the spinach in a small saucepan, sprinkle with a little water and cook for 30–60 seconds, then drain well. Allow all the vegetables to cool, then add them to the batter with the peas and aubergine.
- Heat the oil for deep frying to 180°C/350°F or until a cube of day-old bread browns in about 30 seconds. Drop spoonfuls of the mixture into the hot oil and cook until golden brown. Use a draining spoon to remove the pakoras, then drain them on kitchen paper.
- Keep the cooked pakora hot while cooking the remaining mixture in batches. Serve freshly cooked.

Peppers Baked with Cottage Cheese and Aubergine

Paneer, the Indian unripened cheese often used in vegetarian cookery, is firm and it can be cut into cubes; it is very different from cottage cheese even though it is frequently described as such. One afternoon I popped into one of the many vegetarian restaurants in Colaba, Bombay for a quick snack. When the masala paneer I had ordered arrived, it was served with a rich gravy and the result was delightful. The manager was only too happy to guide me around the kitchens where I was amazed to find that not one of the team could have been much older than 16 (including the manager). In spite of their youth, these chefs were extremely competent and they cooked wonderful food as though from a lifetime of experience. Here, I have spiced cottage cheese as a filling for peppers, topped it with pickle and baked it to make a tempting starter or vegetarian main course.

PREPARATION TIME: 40 MINUTES
COOKING TIME: 20–30 MINUTES
SERVES 6

3 red peppers
2 tablespoons olive oil
1 onion, finely chopped
2 garlic cloves, finely chopped
280g (10oz) cottage cheese
2 green chillies, seeded and finely chopped
2 tomatoes, skinned and finely diced
1 teaspoon cumin powder, roasted (see page 12)
1 tablespoon sultanas
1 tablespoon finely chopped fresh coriander leaves
$^1/_2$ teaspoon salt
8 twists of black pepper
6 teaspoons Brinjal Pickle (see page 179)
1 tablespoon grated Cheddar cheese

To Serve
Clove and Cardamom Dressing (see page 000)
Raita (see page 000)

◆ Preheat the oven to 200°C/400°F/Gas 6. Cut the peppers in half, carefully slicing through the stalks to keep them intact. Remove the seeds and pith.

◆ Heat 1 tablespoon olive oil in a frying pan. Add the onion and garlic, and cook gently for 3–4 minutes, then remove from the heat.

◆ Mix the cottage cheese with the chillies, tomatoes, cumin, sultanas, coriander, salt and black pepper. Stir in the cooked onion and garlic.

◆ Fill the pepper halves with the stuffing mix, then top each with 1 teaspoon brinjal pickle. Drizzle the remaining olive oil over the stuffed peppers and sprinkle with the Cheddar cheese.

◆ Place the peppers in an ovenproof dish and bake for 20–25 minutes, until the peppers are tender and the filling lightly browned. Serve hot, topped with a splash of clove and cardamom dressing, and raita.

Red Lentil Sambar with Urid Dhal Dumplings

One of India's great vegetarian dishes, sambar is cheap and easy to prepare, and it bursts with exotic flavours. Urid dhal dumplings are often served with the sambar. I first tasted this dish in a scruffy little restaurant opposite the Church Gate Railway station in Bombay, an area seething with pandemonium and activity. It seemed fair to bet that everything produced on the subcontinent could be found there, sold by one of the thousands of street hawkers. Exhausted by the heaving crowds, I walked into the first restaurant I found and ordered the sambar with little idea of what to expect.

I was delighted when a bright and colourful dish of lentils and mixed vegetables arrived with a plate of dumplings. Having no notion of the traditional way of eating the dish, I asked the harried waiter for guidance: with a worn look of amusement, and in broken English, he told me to dunk the dumplings in the sambar. So, in they went, one by one soaking up the flavoursome stew, and what a delight they were! Afterwards, I felt completely restored and ready to cope with the trials of Bombay.

SERVES 4
PREPARATION TIME: ABOUT 1 HOUR, PLUS $2^1/2$ HOURS'
SOAKING (OR OVERNIGHT)
COOKING TIME: 35–45 MINUTES

225g (8oz) red lentils
115g (4oz) potatoes, peeled and finely diced
115g (4oz) carrots, finely diced
$^1/2$ teaspoon turmeric
$^1/2$ teaspoon ground cumin
1 teaspoon ground coriander
1 teaspoon Sambar Powder (see page 11)
$1^1/2$ teaspoons salt
2 tablespoons vegetable oil
20 curry leaves

1 teaspoon brown mustard seeds
2 dried red chillies
55g (2oz) frozen peas
1 tablespoon desiccated coconut
2 tablespoons tamarind pulp

Urid Dhal Dumplings
225g (8oz) urid dhal, washed
1 tablespoon chopped fresh coriander leaves
1 mild green chilli, seeded and finely chopped
1 teaspoon salt
vegetable oil for deep-frying

- First soak the urid dhal for the dumplings: place them in a bowl and add 240ml (8fl oz) water. Cover and soak for 2 hours or overnight.
- For the sambar, place the lentils in a small bowl and pour in cold water to cover them. Leave to soak for 15 minutes, then change the water and repeat the soaking. Drain the lentils in a sieve.
- While the lentils are soaking, drain the urid dhal and place them in a blender. Add 120ml (4fl oz) water and blend the dhal to a smooth stiff paste. Turn the paste into a bowl, add the chopped coriander leaves, green chilli and salt, and mix well. Set this paste aside.
- Pour 900ml (1½ pints) water into a saucepan and add the lentils, potatoes, carrots and turmeric. Bring to the boil, reduce the heat so that the water simmers very gently and cook for 25–30 minutes, until the vegetables are tender. Do not over-cook the mixture or the lentils will become very thick and stodgy. Stir in the cumin, coriander, sambar powder and salt.
- Meanwhile, finish making the dumplings towards the end of the cooking time for the sambar. Heat the oil for deep-frying to 190°C/375°F or until a cube of day-old bread browns in about 30 seconds. Use a dessertspoon to add a small amount of the paste to the oil. Cook several dumplings at once, depending on the size of the pan.
- Fry the dumplings for 3 minutes, or until they puff up and turn golden. Drain on kitchen paper and keep hot until the whole

batch is cooked.

♦ Heat a frying pan over medium-high heat and add the 2 tablespoons vegetable oil. When hot, add the curry leaves, mustard
seeds and dried red chillies – they should spit and splutter.
Shake the pan well and fry the spice mixture for 10 seconds,
then add it to the sambar.

♦ Finally, add the peas, coconut and tamarind pulp. Stir well to
thoroughly heat the peas and serve immediately, with the urid
dhal dumplings.

POULTRY & GAME

❖

Winter Chicken with Braised Cabbage and Bacon

In supermarkets, we do not associate food with its farmyard origins, but when I was writing this recipe I thought about the poultry we have kept over many years at Grafton Manor. They were kept for their produce, or for the pot, but there were others, like Hector, a proud and colourful bantam cock with large spurs, strutting about or rousing us with his crowing. One morning, everything was quiet and we were sad, presuming Hector had been taken by a fox. Two days later, hearing rustling coming from an ivy-covered wall, I discovered Hector hanging upside down by his enormous spurs. Back on firm ground, he was very wobbly and undignified, but he lived for many more years into a peaceful old age.

SERVES 4
PREPARATION TIME: 30 MINUTES
COOKING TIME: ABOUT 55 MINUTES

4 tablespoons vegetable oil
1 onion, finely chopped
2 garlic cloves, finely chopped
115g (4oz) smoked bacon, rinded and cut into 2.5cm (1in) strips
1 medium white cabbage, shredded
120ml (4fl oz) Chicken Stock (see page 170)
1 quantity Char-grilled Delhi Chicken (see page 29)
salt

♦ Heat the oil in a saucepan, then add the onion, garlic and bacon. Cook for 3–5 minutes, stirring frequently.
♦ Stir in the cabbage and cook for 5 minutes, then reduce the heat and pour in the chicken stock.
♦ Cook the cabbage gently until it is tender and reduced in volume by about two-thirds – this should take 30–35 minutes.
♦ Add the grilled chicken to the cabbage and heat through, then season to taste with the salt and serve immediately.

Chicken with Crispy Onions

In India, because of the climate, frozen meat and poultry are very popular, but the alternative is a visit to the chicken market. Buying fresh chicken is very unlike a visit to a British butcher, as I discovered in Colaba, a fishing district of Bombay. Although most people prefer not to be reminded that the thing they are cooking or eating was a living creature, there are many who do not have that luxury. The chickens were in pens and the noise was, as you can imagine, incredible. The established practice was to point at your bird, go for a walk and come back 10 minutes later to pick up your poultry. I selected a fat, healthy looking bird with the small privilege of a spacious pen and, I have to admit, there is no substitute in terms of flavour for a bird bought freshly killed. This wonderfully aromatic dish, enlivened with fresh coriander and mint just before serving, is quick and easy to prepare, especially when you do not have to begin at a chicken market.

SERVES 4
PREPARATION TIME: 30 MINUTES
COOKING TIME: 20–30 MINUTES

150ml (5fl oz) vegetable oil
450g (1lb) onions, coarsely chopped
1 teaspoon ground coriander
1 teaspoon ground cumin
1 teaspoon garam masala
$^{1}/_{2}$ teaspoon chilli powder
7.5cm (3in) fresh root ginger, peeled and coarsely chopped
6 garlic cloves
675g (1$^{1}/_{2}$lb) boneless chicken breasts, skinned and cut into 1cm ($^{1}/_{2}$in) dice
$^{1}/_{2}$ tablespoon chopped fresh coriander leaves
$^{1}/_{2}$ tablespoon fresh mint, chopped
$^{1}/_{2}$ teaspoon salt

♦ Heat 6 tablespoons of the oil in a saucepan, add the onions and cook until they are a reddish brown colour. Add the ground spices at this point and remove from the heat. Use a draining spoon to remove a quarter of the onions from the pan and set them aside on a plate.

♦ Place the ginger and garlic in a blender and add 300ml (10fl oz) water. Process until smooth, then pour this mixture into the onions remaining in the pan. Bring back to simmering point and cook very gently for 10–15 minutes, or until the sauce thickens.

♦ Add the chicken and stir well. Simmer for 5–8 minutes, or until the chicken is cooked.

♦ Heat the remaining oil in a frying pan over high heat. Add the reserved onions and re-fry them until they are crisp and dark brown. Using a draining spoon to remove them from the pan and then drain them on kitchen paper to soak up excess oil.

♦ Add the chopped coriander and mint to the chicken and season with salt. Transfer to a serving dish and scatter the crisp onions on top.

Classic Chicken Masala with Peas

The saying 'never judge a book by its cover' should not be applied too rigorously to food as I realised when I was presented with, quite possibly, the worst chicken masala in the world. I unwrapped what I anticipated to be a feast of a take-away and was horrified at what I saw and by the time I had fished out all the pieces of fat, I was left looking at a pile of tripe and bones. So I ordered the same dish from the hotel kitchens and it was superb. This is a classic recipe.

SERVES 4
PREPARATION TIME: 40 MINUTES, PLUS 4–8 HOURS'
MARINATING
COOKING TIME: ABOUT 40 MINUTES

10 black peppercorns
6 cloves
6 green cardamoms
1 cinnamon stick
6 dried red chillies
1¹/₂ teaspoons cumin seeds
5cm (2in) fresh root ginger, peeled and grated
6 garlic cloves, finely chopped
4 chicken legs, skinned and jointed into thighs and drumsticks
6 tablespoons vegetable oil
550g (1¹/₄lb) onions, finely chopped
450ml (15fl oz) plain yogurt
1 teaspoon salt
115g (4oz) frozen peas

◆ Place the peppercorns, cloves, cardamoms, cinnamon, red chillies and cumin seeds in a blender and grind them to a powder. Add the ginger, garlic and 12 tablespoons water, and process the mixture to a paste.
◆ Spread the paste all over the chicken portions and place them

in a bowl. Cover and marinate in the refrigerator for 4–8 hours or overnight.

♦ Heat the oil in a saucepan and fry the onions over high heat until they are red-brown in colour. Reduce the heat to medium and add the chicken. Turn the joints and mix them with the onions, then cook until lightly browned.

♦ Pour in the yogurt and 120ml (4fl oz) water, then increase the heat and bring to the boil. Regulate the heat, if necessary, so that the liquid is just boiling and cook for 15 minutes or until the chicken is tender and cooked through.

♦ Stir in the salt and peas and continue to cook for a further 3 minutes. Serve freshly cooked.

Char-Grilled Chicken with Tomato Butter Sauce

One summer's evening, when Will, my second chef, and I had the evening off, we dashed off to the local supermarket and bought a barbecue kit. It was only when we had assembled the equipment and were full of enthusiasm for christening 'The Grafton Barbecue' that we noticed the absence of charcoal. I decided to use wood, just as they would do in India. At Hyderabad's Hotel Deccan Continental, for instance, they cater for weddings of up to 2000 guests on a daily basis, with much of the food cooked outside over open fires built up with bricks and wood – it makes a fascinating sight.

Our comparatively modest family barbecue was a great success and the meal was rounded with barbecued bananas, my twin sister Nicola's creation. They were wrapped in foil with brandy, butter and sugar, and we ate them from the foil, topped with a large spoonful of whisky cream – heaven!

This chicken dish can be cooked on the barbecue, griddle or griddle pan, or under the grill.

SERVES 4
PREPARATION TIME: 30 MINUTES, PLUS 4–6 HOURS'
MARINATING
COOKING TIME: 6–10 MINUTES

2 cinnamon sticks
10 cloves
12 black peppercorns
10 green cardamoms
$^1/_2$ teaspoon turmeric
7.5cm (3in) fresh root ginger, peeled and chopped
8 garlic cloves, finely chopped
300ml (10fl oz) plain yogurt
juice of $^1/_2$ lemon
1 teaspoon salt
675g (1$^1/_2$1b) boneless chicken breasts, skinned and cut into

2.5cm (1in) cubes
about 1 tablespoon vegetable oil
Tomato Butter Sauce (see page 000) to serve

♦ Grind the cinnamon sticks, cloves, black peppercorns and cardamoms to a powder in a blender. Add the turmeric, ginger,
garlic, yogurt and lemon juice to the spice powder and process
until smooth, then add the salt.
♦ Place the chicken in a deep dish and pour the yogurt mixture
over it. Mix well, then cover and marinate in the refrigerator
for 4–6 hours or overnight.
♦ Lightly grease a grill pan with oil and place the chicken in it,
spreading the pieces out evenly. Cook for 6–10 minutes, turning once, until lightly browned on both sides and just cooked.
Alternatively, the chicken can be cooked on a hot griddle,
either on the hob or on the barbecue.
♦ Serve immediately, with Tomato Butter Sauce (see page 171).

Chicken with Black Pepper and Cardamom

On my next visit to India, I want to spend some time in Madras. Kartic, an Indian friend of mine who now lives near Grafton Manor, is teaching me Hindi. Practising my language skills led to an unfortunate incident last time I went back to India, when I proudly ordered this chicken dish in my best Hindi at one of my favourite restaurants. As the words leaked out, the horrified expression which appeared on the face of the transfixed waiter made me realise that I had made a mistake and had obviously been extremely rude. It took many profuse apologies – in English – to make up for the slip of the tongue.

When I returned to England, I prepared this dish for Kartic, who said that it reminded him of Chicken 65, a Madras dish traditionally served with little steamed rice cakes. I serve Pea, Mushroom and Tomato Curry (see page 128) and Green Chilli and Coriander Chapatis (see page 166) with the chicken as I do not particularly like rice cakes.

SERVES 4
PREPARATION TIME: 1 HOUR, PLUS 8 HOURS' MARINATING
COOKING TIME: 40–45 MINUTES

240ml (8fl oz) plain yogurt
8 garlic cloves
45g (1½ oz) fresh root ginger, peeled and grated
1 tablespoon black peppercorns
25 green cardamoms
1.6kg (3½lb) whole chicken
4 tablespoons vegetable oil
225g (8oz) onion, finely chopped
6 tomatoes, quartered
300ml (10fl oz) whipping cream
1 teaspoon salt
1 tablespoon finely chopped fresh coriander leaves

- Pour the yogurt into a bowl or dish large enough to hold the chicken portions. Place the garlic and ginger in a blender, add 3 tablespoons water and blend to a smooth paste. Stir the paste into the yogurt, then thoroughly wash and dry the blender goblet.
- Grind the black peppercorns and cardamom pods to a powder in the blender, then add them to the yogurt and mix well.
- Skin the chicken, then remove the legs and breasts from the main carcass. Cut the breasts in half and joint the legs into thighs and drumsticks. Add the chicken portions to the yogurt mixture, make sure they are well coated and cover the dish. Set aside in the refrigerator to marinate for 8 hours.
- Heat the vegetable oil in a large saucepan or flameproof casserole. Add the onion and fry for about 5 minutes, or until golden brown. Stir in the tomatoes and cook over low heat for 4–6 minutes, until the tomatoes break up into slightly smaller pieces.
- Add the chicken thighs and drumsticks to the pan with the marinade: the breast portions are added slightly later. Make sure the chicken portions are well coated with the tomato and marinade mixture, and cook for 3–5 minutes. Add the breast portions with any remaining marinade and cook for a further 2–3 minutes.
- Pour in the whipping cream and add the salt. Stir to combine all the ingredients thoroughly, then cover the pan and simmer for 25–30 minutes, or until the chicken is cooked through.
- Finally, add the chopped coriander, stir well and serve.

Note

I prefer to use a whole chicken and joint it into 8 small neat portions; alternatively, you may find it easier to buy ready prepared small chicken portions, such as thighs or drumsticks.

Hyderabadi Chicken Vindaloo

I was introduced to this recipe on a trip to Hyderabad in January 1998. After a six-hour flight delay in Bombay, I jumped into an auto-rickshaw at Hyderabad airport and raced to the Hotel Deccan Continental, which is owned by the friends I was visiting. What I had not realized was that they had reserved the presidential suite for me and when I arrived I felt like a pop star – I was festooned with flowers and greeted by different managers every 5 minutes.

My friends, Lali and Keiran, had planned the whole week and one evening we went to the Hyderabadi Club ('members only', of course) set in a splendid country house for a wonderful dinner with the vice president. Then Lali and I asked if we could work in the kitchens. So the next day was spent with their highly skilled chefs; the chicken vindaloo was the recipe with which I was most impressed. It was nothing like the mouth-roasting firecracker I had expected; made with yellow mustard seeds and a hint of vinegar, the result was not at all hot. It was only then that I realized that a vindaloo is not supposed to burn your mouth to cinders.

I have re-created the dish here: its balance and subtle flavours will be a genuine surprise, giving a whole new meaning to the word 'Vindaloo'. Tomato and Coriander Rice (see page 146) may be served as an accompaniment for the dish.

SERVES 4
PREPARATION TIME: 1 HOUR
COOKING TIME: 45–50 MINUTES

4 chicken legs, including drumsticks and thighs
6 tablespoons vegetable oil
450g (1lb) onions, sliced
225g (8oz) tomatoes, finely diced
30g (1oz) yellow mustard seeds
1 teaspoon turmeric
2 teaspoons ground coriander
1 teaspoon chilli powder

150ml (5fl oz) white wine vinegar
225g (8oz) potatoes, cut into wedges

♦ Cut the chicken portions in half at the joints to separate the thighs and drumsticks.
♦ Heat the vegetable oil in a large saucepan or flameproof casserole. Add the onions, stir well and cook for 15 minutes or until they are reddish-brown in colour.
♦ Add the chicken and cook until lightly browned. Add the tomatoes and stir well, then remove the pan from heat.
♦ Coarsely grind the mustard seeds in a blender and add the coarse powder to the turmeric, ground coriander and chilli powder. Mix to a smooth paste with the vinegar, then pour this paste over the chicken and stir well.
♦ Replace the pan or casserole on medium heat. Add the potatoes and pour in 750ml (1¼ pints) water. Bring to the boil and cook for 5 minutes. Reduce the heat and simmer, uncovered, for a further 25–30 minutes. Season with salt and pepper, and remove from the heat.
♦ To serve, arrange one drumstick and one thigh on each plate and spoon over the sauce. Serve immediately.

Chicken in a Clay Pot

This recipe requires what I call a 'High Street Tandoori' – a clay cooking pot with a lid; the sort of thing that can be purchased from most good kitchenware stores. Cooking in a clay pot is a super way to prepare chicken, but it does require forethought as the pot is soaked in water overnight or for a minimum of 4 hours. Once in the oven, the pot protects the chicken, so there is no need for basting or turning, as when cooking a bird in the usual way. You can do something completely different or go down to the pub for a pre-lunch drink. I well remember one occasion when I tried this leisurely approach and bumped into an old friend with whom I shared a few too many ales. Suddenly, I realized that I had been gone far too long and raced home to be met by clouds of smoke, worse than I had ever seen – it even beat the time when a Spanish guest almost reduced Grafton Manor to ashes!

Serve Mixed Indian Vegetables with Coconut and Coriander (see page 126) with the chicken.

SERVES 4
PREPARATION TIME: ABOUT 30 MINUTES
COOKING TIME: $1^1/4$ HOURS

1.6kg ($3^1/2$lb) chicken
170g (6oz) minced pork (preferably belly pork)
1 onion, finely chopped
6 tablespoons vegetable oil
1 teaspoon coriander seeds
6 cloves
2 bay leaves
4 green cardamoms
4 tablespoons plain yogurt
2 teaspoons turmeric
1 red chilli, seeded and chopped
1 teaspoon ground cumin
2.5cm (1in) fresh root ginger, peeled and grated
4 garlic cloves, finely chopped
salt and black pepper

- Soak a clay cooking pot and its lid overnight in water to cover.
- Skin the chicken and make several cuts across the breasts and thick areas of meat. Mix the pork with half the onion and set it aside.
- Heat 2 tablespoons oil in a frying pan. Add the coriander seeds, cloves, bay leaves and cardamoms, and cook gently until the spices are lightly browned – this should take 2–3 minutes.
- Turn out the spices on to kitchen paper to drain and then mix them into the pork. Season with salt and pepper.
- Stuff the body cavity of the chicken with the pork mixture and place the bird in the drained clay pot.
- Place the yogurt, 1 teaspoon turmeric, red chilli, cumin, ginger and half the chopped garlic in a blender and process the mixture to a smooth paste. Pour this evenly over the chicken.
- Heat the remaining oil in a frying pan. Add the remaining garlic, onion and turmeric, and cook for 2–3 minutes. Purée this mixture in a blender and pour it over the chicken.
- Cover the clay pot and place it in the refrigerator for 2–4 hours to allow the chicken to marinate.
- Preheat the oven to 200°C/400°F/Gas 6. Place the clay pot in the oven and cook the chicken for 1 hour. Remove the lid and cook for 5–10 minutes to brown the chicken.
- Cut the chicken into four portions or carve the meat off the bones, if preferred. Spoon the stuffing on to plates with the chicken and serve immediately.

Chicken with Methi and Dill

Although I disliked the chicken we had for school dinners, when I became a chef I very quickly learned that chicken is a classic, yet versatile, ingredient and discovered how good it tasted with a wide variety of seasonings and other produce. In this recipe the chicken is infused with the methi, fenugreek leaves, and dill, two herbs that complement both the chicken and each other perfectly. Here they are added at the last minute to emphasize their fresh flavours and colour. I tend to grow the herbs and pick them fresh, but you can buy bunches of methi or fenugreek at good Indian grocers. Serve Cauliflower and Asafoetida Purée (see page 125) as an accompaniment.

SERVES 4
PREPARATION TIME: 30–40 MINUTES
COOKING TIME: ABOUT 35 MINUTES

1.35kg (3lb) chicken, cut into 8 pieces, or 8 small chicken
portions, such as thighs, drumsticks or halved breasts
7.5cm (3in) fresh root ginger, peeled and grated
8 garlic cloves
1 teaspoon turmeric
6 tablespoons vegetable oil
450g (1lb) onions, peeled, halved and sliced
300ml (10fl oz) plain yogurt
1 teaspoon salt
3 green chillies, seeded and finely chopped
55g (2oz) fresh methi, chopped
55g (2oz) fresh dill, chopped

♦ Skin the chicken portions and trim off any fat. Put the ginger and garlic in a blender, add 120ml (4fl oz) water and process to a paste. Add the turmeric.

♦ Heat the oil in a saucepan. Add the sliced onions and cook them for 7–10 minutes, until they soften and brown slightly. Stir in the paste, add the chicken and reduce the heat to low, then cook for 10 minutes.

- ◆ Pour in the yogurt and stir in the salt, then cover and cook for a further 10 minutes.
- ◆ Put the green chillies, methi and dill in the rinsed-out blender. Pour in 120ml (4fl oz) water and process until smooth. Add this to the chicken, and simmer for 5 minutes. If you find the sauce is too runny, increase the heat to high and boil the sauce, uncovered, until reduced to a consistency that will coat the back of a spoon. Serve immediately.

Marinated Butter Chicken

William Henderson, my second chef, created this recipe. He spent five weeks in India on a work-experience placement during his hospitality and catering course. Through a friend, I arranged for him to work at the Hotel Deccan Continental in Hyderabad and he quickly fitted into the swing of kitchen work, which is admirable for a seventeen-year-old alone on his first trip across the world.

Indian butter chicken was his favourite dish, but due to the language barrier he was never able to acquire the hotel's recipe. Will searched the curry houses back home in vain for butter chicken to match the one in Hyderabad and eventually concocted his own version of the dish – not the same as the one he tasted in India, but it fills the gap every time that he has a yearning for India and authentic butter chicken.

SERVES 4
PREPARATION TIME: 30 MINUTES, PLUS 24 HOURS'
MARINATING
COOKING TIME: 8–10 MINUTES

450ml (15 fl oz) milk
6 garlic cloves, finely chopped
4 teaspoons ground ginger
4 teaspoons chilli powder
4 teaspoons dried methi
2 teaspoons salt
4 boneless chicken breasts, skinned and cut into 2.5cm (1in) cubes
225g (8oz) butter
4 teaspoons cumin seeds
1 tablespoon tomato purée
4 tablespoons coconut milk
4 tablespoons chopped fresh coriander leaves

◆ Mix the milk, garlic, ginger, chilli powder, methi and salt in a bowl or dish large enough to hold the chicken. Add the chicken, turning the pieces in the marinade to ensure they are all well coated. Cover and place in the refrigerator for up to 24 hours to marinate.

♦ Drain the chicken and reserve the marinade. Melt the butter in a heavy-based saucepan. Add the cumin seeds and chicken. Cook, stirring continuously for about 4 minutes, until the meat is sealed on all sides.

♦ Add the reserved marinade, stir well and simmer over medium heat for 4–6 minutes, or until the chicken is cooked through and tender.

♦ Remove from the heat. Stir in the tomato purée and coconut milk until thoroughly combined, then serve sprinkled with the chopped coriander leaves.

Indian Roast Turkey

A great friend of mine, Lali Nayer, invited me to appear in a television series she was doing for Eastern Mix, an Asian programme. She suggested that I cook an Indian Christmas lunch and after giving it some thought I decided to adapt one of my father's culinary tricks, which is to stuff the turkey under the skin with cream cheese. I infused the cream cheese with spices, giving it a superb flavour and aroma as well as keeping the bird moist during cooking.

Roast Potatoes with Ginger, Garlic and Cardamoms (see page 000) are a great accompaniment. The potatoes retain all their flavour and they are also infused with the range of delicate and tasty spices. The result makes a refreshing change from traditional British roast turkey. Serve Roast Potatoes with Ginger, Garlic and Cardamom (see page 121) and Cabbage with Peas, Cumin and Baby Turnips (see page 132) with the turkey.

SERVES 4
PREPARATION TIME: 45 MINUTES
COOKING TIME: ABOUT $2^3/_4$ HOURS

3.6kg (8lb) turkey
450g (1lb) butter
6 green cardamoms
450g (1lb) cream cheese
3 garlic cloves, finely chopped
2 tablespoons ground coriander
1 tablespoon ground cumin
1 tablespoon turmeric
1 tablespoon cumin seeds
1 teaspoon grated ginger
1 tablespoon ground cinnamon
2 tablespoons finely chopped fresh coriander leaves
2 tablespoons finely chopped fresh mint
salt and black pepper

♦ Preheat the oven to 225°C/425°F/Gas 7. Starting at the neck end of the turkey, use the point of a knife to make a small slit between the skin and meat, taking care not to cut the skin. Using your fingers, and working from the small cut, gradually separate the skin of the bird away from the breast and leg meat. Do not remove or cut the skin: the idea is to create a pocket which can be filled with the cream cheese stuffing. Set the turkey aside.

♦ Melt half the butter, then cool it slightly, if necessary, as it should not be hot enough to melt the cream cheese. Split the cardamom pods, scrape out the tiny seeds and add them to the cream cheese; discard the pods. Mix the melted butter into the cream cheese, then add the garlic, ground coriander, ground cumin, turmeric, cumin seeds, grated ginger and ground cinnamon. Season to taste, mix well and stir in the chopped coriander leaves and mint.

♦ Spoon the cream cheese stuffing into a piping bag fitted with a plain nozzle and carefully insert it between the skin and leg meat of the turkey. Squeeze the mixture into the pocket between the meat and skin, carefully patting it and spreading it to ensure that it covers the flesh evenly. Repeat the process to cover the other leg and the breast meat. Place the prepared turkey in a roasting tin.

♦ Melt the remaining butter. Cut a piece of muslin large enough to cover the whole bird and soak it in the melted butter. Lay this over the top of the turkey to keep it moist during cooking. If you do not have muslin or very fine cotton, brush the butter all over the turkey and cover with foil.

♦ Roast the turkey for 2 hours 40 minutes, or until cooked and golden brown. To check that the meat is cooked through, pierce the thick area on the thigh with the point of a knife: the meat should be firm and look cooked and the juices should be clear. If there is any sign of pink meat or blood in the juices, re-cover the turkey with the muslin or foil and continue cooking, then check again after about 15 minutes.

♦ Remove the muslin and transfer the turkey to a warm serving platter. Carve the turkey and arrange the portions on individual plates. Serve immediately.

Aromatic Turkey

We all seem either to love or hate turkey. My mother does not care for turkey but she does like this dish from the north of India. If you don't like turkey, chicken is a great alternative for this recipe. Serve with Spiced Basmati Rice (see page 144) and Coriander Pesto (see page 173).

SERVES 4
PREPARATION TIME: 30 MINUTES
COOKING TIME: ABOUT 30 MINUTES

4 tablespoons vegetable oil
1.35kg (3lb) turkey breast, cut into 1cm ($^1/_2$in) cubes
10 green cardamoms
10 cloves
1 cinnamon stick or 30g (1oz) cinnamon bark
6 bay leaves
2.5cm (1in) fresh root ginger, peeled and grated
1 garlic clove, finely chopped
240ml (8fl oz) Greek-style yogurt
85g (3oz) raisins
55g (2oz) flaked almonds
salt and black pepper

◆ Preheat the oven to 200°C/400°F/Gas 6. Heat the vegetable oil in a non-stick frying pan over medium heat. Add the turkey and turn the cubes to seal them on all sides – this should take about 3 minutes. Use a draining spoon to transfer the turkey to an ovenproof casserole and set it aside.

◆ Fry the cardamoms, cloves, cinnamon and bay leaves in the oil remaining in the pan for 30 seconds over high heat. Add the ginger and garlic. Cook gently for a further 10 seconds. Stir in the yogurt until well mixed and pour the sauce over the turkey.

◆ Season the turkey and sauce with salt and black pepper, then sprinkle the raisins and flaked almonds over the top. Cover and bake for 20–25 minutes, or until the turkey is cooked through and tender. Serve freshly cooked.

Colonial Turkey Curry

This very British curry, ideal for leftover roast turkey, is a recipe that my mother has been cooking ever since I was a child. It uses curry paste (available from any good supermarket) with raisins, apricots and mango, which are wonderful combined with coconut milk. If you do not have any cooked turkey, the leftovers from any roast poultry will do.

SERVES 4
PREPARATION TIME: 20 MINUTES
COOKING TIME: 25–30 MINUTES

1 tablespoon olive oil
225g (8oz) onions, sliced
2 large garlic cloves, finely chopped
2.5cm (1in) fresh root ginger, peeled and grated
2 tablespoons curry paste
120ml (4fl oz) coconut milk
85g (3oz) ready-to-eat dried apricots, roughly chopped
55g (2oz) ready-to-eat dried mango slices, roughly chopped
30g (1oz) raisins
450g (1lb) cooked turkey, skinned and cut into bite-sized pieces
1 tablespoon Dried Apricot Chutney (see page 178)
1 tablespoon flaked almonds, toasted
1 tablespoon chopped fresh coriander leaves

◆ Heat the oil in a large frying pan. Add the onions and fry for about 15 minutes, or until golden brown. Add the garlic and ginger, and cook for 2 minutes. Stir in the curry paste and cook for 1 minute.

◆ Pour in the coconut milk and stir until it is evenly combined with the curry paste. Reduce the heat to low and simmer for 3 minutes.

◆ Add the apricots, mango, raisins and turkey. Mix well, then simmer for 5 minutes, or until the turkey is thoroughly heated.

◆ Stir in the chutney and serve sprinkled with the toasted almonds and chopped coriander leaves.

Kerala Duck Curry with Black Pepper

Kerala is fast becoming the new holiday paradise of India, rather like Goa was about 10 years ago and it is one of the places I have yet to visit. I met a chef from this southern region and he gave me details of this typical curry from Kerala. It is rich and spicy, using tender duck, black pepper and cashew nuts, and as soon as I tasted it, I understood why he was so keen on passing on the recipe.

I have taken the liberty of adding salami and potatoes to the dish, which makes it a meal in itself; because it is rich, a simple Tomato, Onion and Coriander Salad (see page 138) is the best accompaniment. Roasted Cumin Couscous (see page 135) can also be offered with the duck if a substantial meal is required.

SERVES 4
PREPARATION TIME: 30 MINUTES
COOKING TIME: 35–40 MINUTES

6 tablespoons vegetable oil
30g (1oz) onion, finely chopped
900g (2lb) duck breasts, skinned and cut into 2.5cm (1in) dice
2 tablespoons coriander seeds
5cm (2in) fresh root ginger, peeled and grated
10 garlic cloves, finely chopped
1 teaspoon black peppercorns
6 green cardamoms
3 pieces of cinnamon bark
8 cloves
1 teaspoon chilli powder
2 tablespoons coconut milk
115g (4oz) button mushrooms, quartered
115g (4oz) salami, thinly sliced
15 curry leaves
55g (2oz) cashew nuts
6 small new potatoes, halved
salt and pepper

- ◆ Heat 4 tablespoons vegetable oil in a heavy-based saucepan or flameproof casserole. Add the onion and cook for 3–5 minutes, or until it is red-brown in colour.
- ◆ Add the duck and cook, stirring occasionally, for 3–4 minutes, or until all the pieces are sealed and lightly browned. Meanwhile, grind the coriander seeds to a powder in a blender; set aside.
- ◆ Stir the ginger and garlic into the duck. Reduce the heat to low and add the black peppercorns, cardamoms, cinnamon bark and cloves. Mix well.
- ◆ Add the ground coriander, chilli powder, 600ml (1 pint) water and the coconut milk to the duck. Stir well and increase the heat to high, then cook for 5 minutes. Reduce the heat to low and cook for a further 5 minutes.
- ◆ Heat the remaining vegetable oil in a frying pan. Add the mushrooms and fry for 3 minutes or until lightly browned. Add the salami, curry leaves and cashew nuts. Stir well and cook for a further 2–3 minutes.
- ◆ Add the mushroom and salami mixture to the duck. Stir in the new potatoes and season with salt and pepper. Continue to cook for 8–10 minutes, or until the potatoes are tender. Serve freshly cooked.

Indian Roast Pheasant

When I left school I began a career in gamekeeping, beginning work as a trainee on a local estate. For a gamekeeper, there is a constant supply of pheasants throughout the season, but by the end of January you tire of the familiar dishes. So I spiced up my recipes and now I like to sprinkle cardamom powder over pheasant before roasting it. Here, traditional bread and clove sauce is paired with a reduction of Earl Grey tea and red wine. This subtle spice blend and sauce combination enhances the distinctive flavour of pheasant.

SERVES 4
PREPARATION TIME: 30 MINUTES
COOKING TIME: ABOUT 45 MINUTES

2 dressed pheasants
pinch of salt
2 pinches ground cardamom
10 twists black pepper
2 tablespoons olive oil

Bread and Clove Sauce
115g (4oz) fresh white breadcrumbs
55g (2oz) onion, finely chopped
4 cloves
2 garlic cloves, finely chopped
1 teaspoon cumin seeds, roasted
55g (2oz) butter
450ml (15fl oz) milk
$^1/_2$ teaspoon salt
1 tablespoon chopped fresh coriander leaves

Earl Grey Tea Jus
120ml (4fl oz) red wine
600ml (1 pint) Chicken Stock (see page 170)
2 teaspoons Earl Grey tea leaves

- Preheat the oven to 200°C/400°F/Gas 6. Place the pheasants in a roasting tin and sprinkle with a pinch of salt, the cardamom powder and black pepper. Spoon the olive oil over the pheasants and roast for 10 minutes.

- Turn the birds onto their breasts and roast for another 15 minutes. Remove the pheasants from the oven and allow to rest for 5 minutes.

- Meanwhile, prepare both sauces while the meat is roasting. For the bread sauce put the breadcrumbs, onion, cloves, garlic, cumin seeds, butter and milk into a small saucepan. Bring to the boil over medium heat, stirring often.

- Reduce the heat to low and cook the sauce for 10 minutes, or until it is quite thick, stirring occasionally. Add the salt and chopped coriander.

- For the *jus*, pour the red wine into a saucepan and boil rapidly until it is reduced by half. Add the chicken stock and continue boiling until the liquid is reduced by just over half, to 300ml (10fl oz). Add the Earl Grey tea, reduce the heat and simmer for 5 minutes. Remove from the heat and strain through a fine sieve.

- To serve, spoon the bread sauce on to four plates, discarding the cloves as you do so. Joint each roasted pheasant into four and place a leg and breast on each portion of bread sauce. Pour the tea *jus* around the birds and serve immediately.

Rabbit with Cauliflower and Lentils

Chicken Dansak has been a British curry-house favourite for many years. This dish is similar, but I have used wild rabbit instead of chicken and cauliflower instead of pineapple. Most butchers sell wild rabbit, which has a far superior flavour to that of farmed rabbit. The combination of wild rabbit, lentils and cauliflower makes an excellent, and unusual, winter stew. Courgettes with Tomatoes, Methi and Cumin (see page 130) are the ideal accompaniment.

SERVES 4

PREPARATION TIME: ABOUT 30 MINUTES

COOKING TIME: ABOUT 1 HOUR

4 tablespoons vegetable oil
115g (4oz) onions, finely chopped
1.35kg (3lb) rabbit, prepared and cut into 10 portions
225g (8oz) red lentils
4 garlic cloves, finely chopped
5cm (2in) fresh root ginger, peeled and grated
$1/2$ teaspoon turmeric
$1/2$ teaspoon ground cumin
$1/2$ teaspoon ground coriander
$1/2$ teaspoon chilli powder
$1/2$ teaspoon salt
10 curry leaves
1 teaspoon cumin seeds, roasted (see page 12)
115g (4oz) cauliflower, cut into small florets
1 teaspoon garam masala (see page 8)
1 tablespoon chopped fresh coriander leaves

♦ Heat 3 tablespoons vegetable oil in a saucepan. Add the onions and fry them until they are golden brown.
♦ Add the rabbit portions and fry them until brown and sealed all over, turning often. Mix in the lentils, garlic, ginger, turmeric,

ground cumin, ground coriander and chilli powder.

♦ Pour in 1.4 litres (2¹/₂ pints) water, stir in the salt and bring to the boil. Then reduce the heat and simmer for 35 minutes, or until the rabbit is cooked through and tender.

♦ Heat the remaining vegetable oil over high heat. Add the curry leaves and roasted cumin seeds (they should pop and spit), and fry briefly for 30 seconds. Pour the fried curry leaves and seeds over the rabbit.

♦ Add the cauliflower, cover and cook for a final 10 minutes over low heat, until the cauliflower is tender.

♦ Sprinkle with the garam masala and chopped coriander and serve immediately.

Venison Rogan Josh

I have found many versions of this well-known north Indian dish and this particular interpretation comes from Agra. After visiting all the marble emporia in Agra, I hailed a taxi and set out in search of lunch. Every taxi driver in Agra has a friend who sells the best marble money can buy, all shipped back to your home for a fee of 50 to 100 dollars – paid in advance. I explained that I was more interested in meat than marble and asked if he knew of a place where I could have a good lunch ... of course he did! One of his friends owned a restaurant which served a good rogan josh – dark, rich, and full of northern spices – enough even to wipe away my marble blues. I acquired the recipe and I have refined it a little, using the richer flavour of venison instead of lamb. The venison is perfect with the other full-flavoured ingredients.

SERVES 4–6
PREPARATION TIME: 20 MINUTES
COOKING TIME: ABOUT 1 1/4 HOURS

8 black cardamoms
12 green cardamoms
10cm (4in) cinnamon stick
15 black peppercorns
6 tablespoons vegetable oil
900g (2lb) boneless venison, cut into 1cm (1/2in) cubes
5 onions, sliced
20 garlic cloves, finely chopped
10cm (4in) fresh root ginger, peeled and grated
2 tablespoons paprika
1/2 tsp chilli powder
1 tablespoon ground coriander
1 1/2 tsp salt

♦ Heat a small frying pan. Add the black and green cardamoms, cinnamon and black peppercorns. Roast the spices for 10–20 seconds, until they are lightly browned, then grind them to a fine powder in a blender.

- ◆ Heat the oil in a saucepan over a high heat and fry the venison, stirring and turning the pieces occasionally, until evenly browned.
- ◆ Add the onions and fry for 5 minutes, or until they are well browned. Stir in the garlic and ginger, and cook for a further 3 minutes.
- ◆ Reduce the heat to low and add the ground roast spices with the paprika, chilli powder and ground coriander. Mix well.
- ◆ Pour in 600ml (1 pint) water and stir in the salt. Bring to the boil, then reduce heat to low again and simmer the venison for 55 minutes, or until it is tender and the sauce has thickened.
- ◆ If the sauce is not thick enough at the end of cooking, increase the heat and boil to reduce the liquid and give a smooth consistency. Serve piping hot.

Meat

❖

Hyderabadi Lamb with Rice and Peas

Being the one which secured the 'Curry Chef of the Year' award in 1997, this recipe has to be one of my favourites. I learnt how to cook it at the Taj Hotel in Hyderabad and it has featured high in my repertoire ever since because I think it demonstrates Indian cuisine at its best. The meat is marinated in a marvellous blend of spices and then sealed in the cooking pot until superbly succulent. Finally, peas are added at the last moment, retaining their freshness and enhancing both the appearance and flavour of the dish. It is truly one of Hyderabad's culinary masterpieces.

SERVES 4
PREPARATION TIME: 30 MINUTES, PLUS 4–12 HOURS'
MARINATING
COOKING TIME: ABOUT 1^{1}/$_{4}$ HOURS

1.1kg (2^{1}/$_{2}$lb) shoulder of lamb, boned and cut into 1cm (^{1}/$_{2}$in) cubes
300ml (10fl oz) plain yogurt
1 teaspoon turmeric
2 teaspoons chilli powder
1 cinnamon stick
6 green cardamoms
6 cloves
8 garlic cloves
7.5cm (3in) fresh root ginger, coarsely chopped
1 teaspoon salt
6 tablespoons vegetable oil
225g (8oz) onions, halved and sliced
55g (2oz) basmati rice
115g (4oz) frozen peas, thawed
1 tablespoon chopped fresh coriander leaves
2 tablespoons coconut milk
2 tablespoons double cream
sealing paste

225g (8oz) plain flour

♦ Place the diced lamb in a bowl. Add the yogurt, turmeric and chilli powder, and mix well. Then add the cinnamon stick, cardamoms and cloves, and mix well again.

♦ Place the garlic and ginger in a blender and pour in just enough water to cover them, then process the mixture to a thin paste. Pour this over the lamb, add the salt and mix well. Cover and set aside in the refrigerator to marinate for 4–12 hours.

♦ Heat the oil in a large heavy-based saucepan. Add the sliced onions and cook them until they are golden brown, stirring occasionally. Add the lamb and cook for 3 minutes, then stir in the rice and reduce the heat to low.

♦ Make the paste to seal the saucepan: place the flour in a bowl and add (75ml) 2½fl oz water. Mix the water into the flour to form a dough, then knead briefly until smooth and roll it into a sausage-shape.

♦ Press the dough around the rim of the saucepan. Place the saucepan lid on top, pressing it down on to the dough to create an airtight seal. Cook over low heat for 55–60 minutes.

♦ Remove the pan from the heat and use a knife to break the dough seal, then remove the lid. Add the peas, chopped coriander, coconut milk and cream. Mix well to heat the peas through. Serve immediately.

Lamb with Chick Peas and Couscous

Lamb is such a traditional British ingredient that when I first started experimenting by adding Indian spices to it I felt as though I was committing sacrilege. I quickly realized that spices add to the strong flavour of lamb, rather than detracting from it, giving an overall result that is more subtle than a traditional roast.

I use boned shoulder of lamb for this dry curry, combining it with chick peas and infusing it with the spices that are popular in north Indian cooking, where wonderful aromas combine with intense flavours. Adding couscous right at the end of the cooking captures the moisture and completes the succulent dish. Serve Naan Bread (see page 167) and Buttered Almond and Raisin Rice (see page 147) with the lamb.

SERVES 4
PREPARATION TIME: 20 MINUTES, PLUS OVERNIGHT
SOAKING
COOKING TIME: 45 MINUTES, PLUS 10 MINUTES' STANDING

3 tablespoons vegetable oil
675g (1^1/$_2$lb) boneless shoulder of lamb, cut into 2.5cm (1in) cubes
1 onion, finely chopped
3 garlic cloves, finely chopped
1 cinnamon stick, broken into 4 pieces
2 teaspoons dried methi
1 teaspoon cumin seeds, roasted (see page 12)
55g (2oz) drained canned chick peas
30g (1oz) couscous
1 teaspoon salt

♦ Heat the oil in a large saucepan over high heat. Add the lamb and lightly brown the pieces, turning occasionally.
♦ Add the onion and garlic. Stir well, reduce the heat to medium and cook for 3–5 minutes. Mix in the cinnamon, methi, cumin

seeds and chick peas. Then pour in 120ml (4fl oz) water and bring to the boil.

♦ Reduce the heat to low, cover the pan and cook slowly for 40 minutes, or until the lamb is tender. By the time the meat is cooked, the water should have evaporated leaving the dish moist, but not wet. If necessary, increase the heat and cook uncovered until excess liquid has evaporated.

♦ Add the couscous and salt, and mix in well. Cover and remove from the heat, then leave to stand for 10 minutes before serving.

Lamb Cooked with Spinach, Baby Turnips and Ginger

Major, my black labrador, leads a life of luxury, with his own detached residence, 4 acres of lawns and a $2^{1}/_{2}$ acre lake in which to swim or chase ducks (his preferred summer pastime). Everyone at Grafton knows that his favourite food is curry, but he is fussy: he will only eat potatoes if they are peeled and whole tomatoes are definitely not acceptable on his menu. However, Major loves this particular dish – as long as the baby turnips are removed. I like to serve Goan Bread Rolls (page 162) or Spiced Basmati Rice (page 144) as accompaniments.

SERVES 4
PREPARATION TIME: 45 MINUTES, PLUS 2–4 HOURS'
MARINATING
COOKING TIME: ABOUT 2 HOURS

675g ($1^{1}/_{2}$ lb) boneless shoulder of lamb, plus bones
450g (1lb) onions
6 tablespoons vegetable oil
6 green cardamoms
240ml (8fl oz) plain yogurt
45g ($1^{1}/_{2}$oz) fresh root ginger, peeled
6 garlic cloves, crushed
1 teaspoon chilli powder
$^{1}/_{2}$ teaspoon turmeric
2 teaspoons ground coriander
10 baby turnips
340g (12oz) spinach
1 teaspoon salt
1 tablespoon chopped fresh coriander leaves

◆ Trim the lamb of excess fat and save any scraps. Chop 1 onion. Heat 1 tablespoon of the oil in a large saucepan. Add the lamb bones, meat trimmings and chopped onion, and cook until browned, turning the bones occasionally. Pour in enough water to cover the bones, bring to the boil and reduce the heat. Simmer for 30 minutes. Strain the stock and skim off any fat.

♦ Cut the lamb into 1cm (^{1}/$_2$in) cubes and place in a bowl. Add the cardamoms. Pour the yogurt into a blender. Roughly chop two-thirds of the ginger and add it to the yogurt with the garlic, chilli powder and turmeric, then blend the mixture to a smooth paste. Pour this paste over the lamb, cover and place in the refrigerator to marinate for 2–4 hours or overnight.

♦ Cut the remaining onions in half and slice them finely. Heat 4 tablespoon oil in a heavy-based saucepan or flameproof casserole and add the onions. Fry the onions until they are golden brown. Stir in the ground coriander and turnips.

♦ Stir in the lamb and cook over a low heat for 3 minutes. Pour in 600ml (1 pint) of the lamb stock and bring to the boil. Cover and reduce the heat, then simmer for 55–60 minutes, or until the meat is tender.

♦ Remove the lid from the pan or casserole and bring the lamb to the boil, then boil fast for 5 minutes to reduce the quantity of liquid and make a smooth, thick sauce.

♦ Reduce the heat and add the spinach but do not mix it into the meat. Cover and cook for another 5 minutes, until the spinach has wilted. Thoroughly mix the spinach with the lamb and add the salt.

♦ Cut the remaining ginger into fine matchstick strips and fry them in the remaining oil until golden brown. Scatter the ginger and chopped coriander leaves over the lamb and serve immediately.

Lamb with Coconut Milk and Curry Leaves

Bangalore, the capital city of Karnataka, is the prosperous computer capital of India. However, apart from one very good restaurant, I found the food to be a little disappointing. The 'Coconut Grove' is a plush open-air restaurant which served excellent food when I visited. I tried an executive lunch thali, with six vegetarian dishes, three meat dishes and two sweets. This lamb dish, one of the meat dishes on the thali, apparently originates from the first-class buffet carriage on trains of a bygone era. Karnataka is a large coconut-growing state, so coconut milk is used extensively in the region's cookery and this dish is a fine example of the cuisine. Serve Buttered Almond and Raisin Rice (see page 147) as an accompaniment.

SERVES 4
PREPARATION TIME: 30 MINUTES
COOKING TIME: ABOUT 50 MINUTES

4 tablespoons vegetable oil
2 teaspoons cumin seeds
225g (8oz) onions, finely chopped
900g (2lb) boneless shoulder of lamb, cut into 1cm ($^1/_2$in) cubes
8 garlic cloves, finely chopped
5cm (2in) fresh root ginger, grated
$^1/_2$ teaspoon nigella seeds
3 small dried red chillies
2 teaspoons ground coriander
12 fresh or dried curry leaves
8 new potatoes, cut into 1cm ($^1/_2$in) cubes
8 baby carrots or medium carrots, cut into 1cm ($^1/_2$in) cubes
8 baby turnips or medium turnips, cut into 1cm ($^1/_2$in) cubes
300ml (10fl oz) chicken stock or water
175ml (6fl oz) coconut milk
1 teaspoon salt
1 tablespoon chopped fresh coriander leaves

◆ Heat the vegetable oil in a saucepan. Add the cumin seeds and onions, and fry for 5–8 minutes or until the onions are lightly browned. Add the lamb and cook, stirring continuously, until the pieces are sealed on all sides. Add the garlic and ginger, and fry for another 3 minutes.

◆ Stir in the nigella seeds, red chillies, ground coriander and curry leaves. Add the potatoes, carrots, turnips and chicken stock or water. Bring to the boil, then immediately reduce the heat and simmer for 10 minutes.

◆ Pour in the coconut milk and simmer for a further 25 minutes or until the meat and vegetables are tender. If the sauce is too thin, increase the heat to high and boil the curry until the liquid has reduced and the sauce is thick enough to coat the back of a spoon.

◆ Finally, add the salt and chopped coriander leaves and serve immediately.

Lamb with Tomato and Potatoes

I love the combination of the tender lamb and potatoes with sweet tomatoes in this dish. If possible, use waxy potatoes as they retain their texture during cooking.

SERVES 4
PREPARATION TIME: 20 MINUTES
COOKING TIME: ABOUT 1^1/$_2$ HOURS

1 teaspoon cumin seeds
1 teaspoon coriander seeds
8 cloves
3 dried red chillies
8 tablespoons vegetable oil
225g (8oz) onions, finely chopped
6 garlic cloves, finely chopped
5cm (2in) fresh root ginger, peeled and grated
900g (2lb) shoulder of lamb, boned and cut into 1cm (^{1}/$_2$in) cubes
6 pieces cinnamon bark
450g (1lb) tomatoes, quartered
450g (1lb) potatoes, cut into 1cm (^{1}/$_2$in) cubes
1 teaspoon salt

◆ Heat a small frying pan over high heat. Add the cumin seeds and coriander seeds, cloves and dried red chillies, and roast for 20–30 seconds. Cool for a few seconds, then grind to a fine powder in a blender.

◆ Heat the oil in a saucepan. Add the onions and fry them until they are a red-brown colour. Add the garlic, ginger and ground spices. Stir well and cook for 2 minutes.

◆ Add the lamb and cinnamon bark to the onion mixture, then cook for 5 minutes, stirring frequently. Stir in the tomatoes and reduce the heat to low. Cook, stirring occasionally, until the tomatoes are well broken down.

◆ Pour in 600ml (1 pint) water and bring to the boil, then cook for 5 minutes. Reduce the heat to low, cover and simmer gently for 40 minutes.

♦ Stir in the potatoes, add the salt and cook for a further 25 minutes, or until the potatoes are tender. Serve freshly cooked.

Lamb with Yogurt and Roasted Spices

Long marinating in yogurt with ginger and garlic imparts a marvellous flavour and succulent texture to lamb. It is the perfect approach for slightly fatty shoulder and the result is a superbly tasty dish. I like to serve Chick Pea and Lentil Curry (see page 154) as an accompaniment.

SERVES 4

PREPARATION TIME: 20 MINUTES, PLUS 4 HOURS'
MARINATING

COOKING TIME: ABOUT 1 HOUR

6 green cardamoms
8 cloves
5cm (2in) piece cinnamon bark
3 dried red chillies
1 tablespoon coriander seeds
240ml (8fl oz) plain yogurt
5cm (2in) fresh root ginger, peeled and finely chopped
4 garlic cloves, finely chopped
900g (2lb) shoulder of lamb, boned and cut into 2.5cm (1in)
cubes
6 tablespoons vegetable oil
340g (12oz) onions, finely chopped

♦ Heat a small frying pan over high heat. Add the cardamoms, cloves, cinnamon bark, chillies and coriander seeds, and roast for 30 seconds or until they are lightly browned. Quickly remove them from the heat and grind them to a fine powder in a blender.

♦ Pour the yogurt into a bowl or dish large enough to hold the lamb. Stir in the ginger and garlic, then add the lamb and mix well. Cover and place in the refrigerator to marinate for 4 hours or overnight.

♦ Heat the oil in a saucepan over medium-high heat. Add the

onions and fry them until they are golden brown. Stir in the ground spices and cook for 3 minutes, then reduce the heat to low and cook, stirring continuously, for a further 3 minutes.

♦ Add the lamb with all the marinade and stir well. Cook for 5 minutes, then pour in 600ml (1 pint) water and bring to the boil. Reduce the heat and simmer for 40 minutes, or until the meat is tender and the sauce has thickened.

♦ Stir in the salt and serve piping hot.

Traditional Mutton Curry

In India, the bones are used with the meat when making curries. This improves the flavour and it also reduces the food costs in a restaurant, an important consideration when resources are at a premium. Mutton has a stronger taste than lamb, which is under 12 months old; I prefer to use only best-quality mutton in my curries, since this is the best way to ensure that the dish has a distinctive flavour and excellent meat. Bird's eye chillies are tiny and fiery in flavour – if you cannot find them, use 2 larger red chillies instead. I always enjoy cooking this great old dish, and like to serve Green Chilli and Coriander Chapatis (see page 166) and Fragrant Sweetcorn Rice (see page 145) as side dishes.

SERVES 4

PREPARATION TIME: 30 MINUTES, PLUS 2–4 HOURS'
SOAKING

COOKING TIME: ABOUT $1^1/_4$ HOURS

90g (3oz) desiccated coconut
500ml (17fl oz) milk
6 dried birds eye chillies
4 pieces cinnamon bark
6 cloves
1 teaspoon cumin seeds
6 tablespoons vegetable oil
450g (1lb) onions, finely chopped
2.5cm (1in) fresh root ginger, peeled and grated
4 large garlic cloves, finely chopped
4 teaspoons paprika
3 teaspoons ground coriander
2 bay leaves
900g (2lb) boneless mutton or leg of lamb, cut into 1cm ($^1/_2$in) cubes
225g (8oz) tomatoes, quartered
1 teaspoon salt

♦ Place the coconut in a basin, pour in the milk and leave to soak for 2–4 hours. At the end of the soaking time, strain the milk through a fine sieve, pressing as much moisture as possible from the coconut.

- Meanwhile, roast the chillies, cinnamon bark, cloves and cumin seeds together in a heavy-based frying pan for 30 seconds, then grind the spices to a powder in a blender.

- Heat the oil in a large saucepan. Add the onions and fry them until they are golden brown, stirring occasionally. Stir in the ginger and garlic, and cook for 3 minutes. Then add the paprika, coriander, ground roasted spices and bay leaves. Stir well and pour in the coconut milk.

- Add the mutton or lamb, 600ml (1 pint) water and the tomatoes. Bring to the boil, stirring, and cook for 5 minutes. Reduce the heat so that the curry simmers steadily and cook for 45–50 minutes, or until the meat is tender.

- If the sauce is too thin when the meat is cooked, increase the heat and boil the sauce so that excess liquid evaporates and it becomes thick and creamy. Stir in the salt and serve immediately.

Goan Pork Sorpatel

Wherever you eat in Goa, you are always sure to find this dish, one of the region's culinary classics. One of the best sorpatels I have ever eaten was at the house of some friends in Mapusa. I had been invited to a holy day celebration at their Roman Catholic church and the scene that greeted me was vibrant and colourful. Everyone was dressed in Sunday best and we all congregated in a large and airy chapel for the service, relieved to shelter from the oppressive heat outside. I imagined that the day would be taken up with thoughtful prayer, so was surprised to discover that mass was followed by fun celebrations, first the Indian equivalent of bingo, and then a feast of a meal.

Most families keep pigs especially for occasions like this, when only the fattest are slaughtered for the meal. The pigs are fed with the best of the scraps to ensure that no-one will go hungry when the great day comes. I felt honoured and extremely lucky to be included in the family gathering where we all happily ate our fill from huge pots of pork curry. There were bowls of mixed salad and basmati rice, and crates of Kingfisher beer to wash down the food.

SERVES 4

PREPARATION TIME: 30 MINUTES, PLUS 2–4 HOURS'
MARINATING

COOKING TIME: ABOUT 1 HOUR

4 dried red chillies
4 cloves
3 green cardamoms
2 teaspoons black peppercorns
1 teaspoon cumin seeds
$^1/_2$ teaspoon turmeric
1 tablespoon white wine vinegar
900g (2lb) boneless leg of pork, cut into 2.5cm (1in) cubes
4 tablespoons vegetable oil
225g (8oz) onions, finely chopped
7.5cm (3in) fresh root ginger, peeled and grated

4 garlic cloves, finely chopped
115g (4oz) tomatoes, roughly chopped
225g (8oz) pig's liver, trimmed and sliced
2 pig's kidneys, cored and cut into 1cm ($^1/_2$in) cubes
1 teaspoon salt

♦ Heat a small frying pan over high heat. Add the dried red chillies, cloves, green cardamoms, black peppercorns and cumin
seeds, and roast for 30 seconds. Then grind to a powder in a
blender.

♦ Add the turmeric, vinegar and 3 tablespoons water to the
ground spices and continue to process until they form a paste.

♦ Place the pork in a bowl or dish and add the paste. Mix well to
coat all the pieces of meat with paste, then cover the dish and
marinate the meat in the refrigerator for 2–4 hours, or
overnight.

♦ Heat the oil in a saucepan. Add the onions and cook until they
are golden brown. Stir in the ginger and garlic, and cook for 3–5
minutes. Add the tomatoes and cook for a further 5 minutes,
stirring continuously.

♦ Add the pork and all the marinade to the pan. Mix well and
pour in 600ml (1 pint) water. Bring to the boil and cook for 3
minutes. Reduce the heat and simmer the curry gently for 40
minutes.

♦ Add the liver and kidneys, and mix well. Cook for a further 5
minutes, or until the liver and kidneys are just cooked. Gently
mix in the salt and serve immediately.

Pork with Honey, Mustard and Fresh Coriander

We remember meals we first knew and loved as children. Unusually, as a child I always preferred savoury food – this was probably the result of having a father who was a chef. This recipe stands out in my memory, probably because of the blend of sweet and savoury. The honey offsets the rich savoury flavours of pork and mustard. My father has been cooking this recipe for years; it is not exactly Indian, but it is so good that I thought I would include it. The secret is to cook the harshness out of the mustard and to add coriander – the Indian ingredient – right at the end to preserve its fresh flavour.

SERVES 6
PREPARATION TIME: 20 MINUTES
COOKING TIME: 1 HOUR 50 MINUTES

4 tablespoons clear honey
4 tablespoons Dijon mustard
3 tablespoons vegetable oil
10 twists black pepper
1.35kg (3lb) loin of pork, boned and skinned
300ml (10fl oz) Chicken Stock (see page 170)
240ml (8fl oz) whipping cream
1 tablespoon chopped fresh coriander leaves

♦ Preheat the oven to 200°C/400°F/Gas 6. Mix the honey, mustard, oil and black pepper in a small bowl to make a smooth sauce.
♦ Cut two 35cm- (14in-) long sheets of foil and lay one on top of the other. Place the pork on the foil and rub a generous tablespoonful of the honey sauce all over the meat. Then fold the foil around the pork and pinch the edges together to seal the meat in a neat parcel.
♦ Place the pork parcel on a baking tray and cook in the preheated oven for 1 hour.

- Pour the remaining sauce in a saucepan and bring to the boil. Reduce the heat, stir in the chicken stock and simmer gently for 30 minutes. This removes the bitterness from the mustard and makes the sauce smooth. Add the cream and simmer for a further 10 minutes.
- Open the top of the foil parcel and cook the pork for another 10 minutes to brown the top of the joint. Allow the meat to rest for 10 minutes after removing it from the oven.
- Carve the pork into 5mm ($^{1}/_{4}$in) slices and arrange them on a platter or individual plates. Stir the chopped coriander leaves into the sauce and pour it over the pork. Serve immediately.

Tandoori Lamb's Liver

I savour the heavy, intense flavour of liver and so I decided to cook this dish, which blends traditional English ingredients with Indian spices, for good friends who were visiting from India. As the distinctive odour of liver wafted over from the kitchen, my guests gave me askance looks. They had anticipated eccentricity at Grafton Manor, but now they feared they smelled a rotten joke. However, when this superb dish was served, they all agreed that it was definitely one to add to the collection.

Always use the freshest liver for this recipe and marinate it for up to 24 hours before cooking it to your liking. Indian Mashed Potatoes (see page 120) and Coriander Pesto (see page 173) are delicious with the liver.

SERVES 6
PREPARATION TIME: 15 MINUTES, PLUS 4 HOURS'
MARINATING
COOKING TIME: 20–35 MINUTES

6 × 170g (6oz) pieces lamb's liver
600ml (1 pint) plain yogurt
5 garlic cloves, finely chopped
5cm (2in) fresh root ginger, peeled and finely grated
2 teaspoons ground cardamom
2 teaspoons paprika
2 teaspoons garam masala (see page 8)
2 green chillies, seeded and chopped
1 scant teaspoon salt
6 sprigs of mint
30g (1oz) fresh coriander leaves
2 tablespoons olive oil

♦ Score the top of the liver in a criss-cross pattern and lay the pieces in a dish.
♦ Pour the yogurt into a blender. Add the garlic, ginger, ground cardamom, paprika and garam masala, and process for 3 seconds. Add the salt, mint and coriander and process for 1

minute, or until smooth.

♦ Pour the yogurt mixture over the liver and turn the pieces to make sure that they are evenly coated. Cover and marinade in the refrigerator for 4 hours or overnight.

♦ Preheat the oven to 200°C/400°F/Gas 6. Brush an ovenproof dish or roasting tin with olive oil and add the liver, with the marinade. Bake the liver for 20–25 minutes, when the liver will be pink in the middle. If you prefer liver well cooked, then cook for a further 5–10 minutes. Serve immediately.

Fish & Seafood

❖

Goan Fish Curry

After working in Bombay, I spent a week on holiday in Goa. I arrived and headed straight down to the beach for a relaxing afternoon, then drifted off to sleep in the sun. Two hours later I was the colour of a Cornish lobster and well cooked; with my feet about double their normal size, I just about managed to hobble back to my hotel. As I was applying after-sun cream the room-service attendant knocked to see if I wanted anything. He took one look at my feet, dashed off and returned with one of his father's remedies – hot water mixed with masses of tamarind leaves, which he dabbed over my feet. It was extremely painful, but it did relieve the sunburn. Since I could not make it to the restaurant for dinner, he came back later with a large bowl of steaming fish curry and plain rice. This kindness is typical of Indian people.

SERVES 4
PREPARATION TIME: 35 MINUTES.
COOKING TIME: 20 MINUTES

10 dried red chillies
5 teaspoons coriander seeds
5 teaspoons cumin seeds
1 teaspoon black peppercorns
1 teaspoon paprika
1 teaspoon turmeric
10 garlic cloves
5cm (2in) fresh root ginger, peeled and grated
5 tablespoons vegetable oil
225g (8oz) onions, finely chopped
225g (8oz) tomatoes, quartered
200ml (7fl oz) coconut milk
900g (2lb) pomfret or red snapper fillets
1 teaspoon salt
2 tablespoons tamarind pulp (see page 12)
1 tablespoon chopped fresh coriander leaves

- Process the chillies, coriander, cumin, black peppercorns, paprika and turmeric to a powder in a blender. Add the garlic, ginger and 12 tablespoons water and process again to form a paste.
- Heat the oil in a saucepan over high heat. Add the onions and cook until they are golden brown, stirring often. Reduce the heat to medium, add the tomatoes and cook until they have broken up.
- Stir in the spice paste until well mixed and cook for 5 minutes. Pour in 240ml (8fl oz) water and the coconut milk. Bring to the boil and cook for 3–5 minutes, then reduce the heat so that the sauce simmers. The sauce should have a light consistency.
- Cut the fish across into 5cm (2in) slices and add them to the curry sauce. Cook gently for 5 minutes, or until the fish is just firm and opaque.
- Add the salt, tamarind pulp and chopped coriander, mix carefully, to avoid breaking up the fish, and cook for a final 3 minutes. Serve immediately.

Juhu Tara Road Fish Curry

In Juhu, a relatively wealthy suburb of Bombay, I came across a wonderful street restaurant on the busy Tara Road, a main thoroughfare. The restaurant obviously had a lot of good custom from businessmen and workers alike, which did not seem surprising when I tasted their fish curry, made from pomfret and shark. The fish was beautifully light and infused with paprika, turmeric, fresh curry leaves and tomatoes; it was served in shallow stainless steel bowls with plain rice and pao (small white bread rolls) to mop up the aromatic sauce.

SERVES 4
PREPARATION TIME: 35 MINUTES
COOKING TIME: 35–40 MINUTES

5 tablespoons vegetable oil
2 onions, finely chopped
5cm (2in) fresh root ginger, peeled and grated
3 garlic cloves, crushed
1 tablespoon paprika
1 tablespoon ground coriander
1 tablespoon ground cumin
$^1/_2$ teaspoon turmeric
$^1/_2$ teaspoon chilli powder
20 curry leaves
300ml (10fl oz) coconut milk
2 tablespoons tamarind pulp (see page 12)
$1^1/_2$ teaspoons salt
20 mussels, scrubbed and beards removed
12 tiger prawns, peeled, preferably uncooked, thawed if frozen
450g (1lb) shark or huss fillet, skinned and cut into chunks
450g (1lb) salmon fillet, skinned and cut into chunks
1 tablespoon chopped fresh coriander leaves

◆ Heat the oil in a large saucepan. Add the onions and cook, stirring, for about 10 minutes, or until they are red-brown. Add the ginger and garlic, and cook for a further 3 minutes.

- Stir in the paprika, ground coriander, cumin, turmeric and chilli powder, and cook for 2 minutes. Then pour in 1.2 litres (2 pints) water and add the curry leaves. Bring to the boil and cook for about 10 minutes, or until the sauce has reduced by half. Pour in the coconut milk, add the tamarind pulp and salt; stir well and reduce the heat to low. Simmer gently for 5 minutes.
- Meanwhile, discard any mussels that do not close when tapped with the handle of a spoon or knife. Add the mussels, prawns, shark or huss and salmon to the curry sauce and continue simmering for 5–8 minutes, or until the mussels have opened and the prawns and fish are cooked.
- Check the mussels and discard any that have not opened. Finish by sprinkling with the chopped fresh coriander. Serve immediately.

Red Snapper with Tamarind

Red snapper is a good meaty fish, often to be found in the waters of the Indian Ocean. Mackerel can be used instead, if preferred. The sourness of the tamarind in this recipe is offset by the infusion of garlic, ginger and coriander. Cauliflower and Potato Curry (see page 124) or Tomato, Onion and Coriander Salad (see page 138) are ideal accompaniments.

SERVES 4
PREPARATION TIME: 15 MINUTES
COOKING TIME: 20–30 MINUTES

4 tablespoons tamarind pulp
$^1/_2$ onion, finely chopped
1 large green chilli, seeded and finely chopped
3 garlic cloves, finely chopped
5cm (2in) fresh root ginger, peeled and grated
$^1/_2$ teaspoon salt
1 tablespoon chopped fresh coriander leaves
grated rind of 1 lime and juice of $^1/_2$ lime
5 tablespoons olive oil
4 × 170g (6oz) red snapper fillets

♦ Preheat an oven to 180°C/350°F/Gas 4. Thoroughly mix the tamarind, onion, chilli and garlic. Add the ginger, salt, chopped coriander, lime rind and juice. Stir the mixture well until the ingredients are evenly mixed in a thick paste, then stir in 4 tablespoons of olive oil.

♦ Brush the remaining olive oil over an ovenproof dish that can be placed under the grill and lay the snapper fillets in it, skin side down. Brush the tamarind mixture over the fish, reserving any excess, and bake for 20–25 minutes, until just cooked. Baste the fillets with any remaining tamarind mixture halfway through the cooking process.

♦ Preheat the grill just before the fish have finished baking. Grill the fish for 1–2 minutes to lightly brown the tops of the fillets. Serve immediately.

Salmon with Spinach and Coriander

When I'm in Juhu, Bombay, I always go to the Hotel Sea Princess and pay the modest fee for the use of their lovely pool instead of dipping in the sea. On one occasion I noticed that there was a buffet lunch laid out and the duty manageress kindly explained the array of dishes. The swimming had given me an appetite and the selection of food was mouthwatering, so I persuaded the lady to allow me to sample a spinach, coriander and sweetcorn dish. I was so impressed that I asked her for the recipe.

When I brought it back to England, I decided to turn it into a more substantial dish. I added a little succulent salmon and discovered that the delicate flavours blended perfectly. The pink of the salmon contrasted beautifully with the green spinach and, with the irresistible aroma, it became a dish to satisfy all senses. Buttered Almond and Raisin Rice (see page 147) may be offered as an accompaniment.

SERVES 4
PREPARATION TIME: 35 MINUTES
COOKING TIME: 20–30 MINUTES

450g (1lb) spinach
4 tablespoons vegetable oil
1 small onion, finely chopped
4 garlic cloves, finely chopped
1 teaspoon cumin seeds, roasted (see page 000)
55g (2oz) drained canned or frozen sweetcorn
2 bay leaves
150ml (5fl oz) coconut milk
1 teaspoon salt
675g (1¹/₂lb) salmon fillet, skinned and cut into 1cm (¹/₂in) cubes
1 tablespoon chopped fresh coriander leaves

♦ Half fill a medium saucepan with water and bring it to the boil. Add the spinach and cook for 3 minutes, then turn the spinach into a colander and leave it to drain well for 3–5 minutes.

♦ Heat the vegetable oil in the saucepan. Add the onion, garlic and roasted cumin seeds and cook, stirring occasionally, for about 10 minutes, or until the onion has softened and browned slightly.

♦ Meanwhile, purée the drained spinach in a blender until smooth, then add it to the onion mixture with the sweetcorn, bay leaves and coconut milk. Stir well and cook over low to medium heat for 3–5 minutes.

♦ Stir in the salt and add the salmon, then cook for 5–8 minutes. Finally, stir in the chopped coriander and serve.

Spicy Cod in a Parcel

Any white fish may be used for this recipe. The fish is marinated in yogurt, wrapped in greaseproof paper with a whole green chilli and then baked. The flavours are quite different from those you might normally associate with cod and the yogurt marinade creates a style and texture as characteristic of the dish as the flavour. Unlike chopped chilli, the whole chilli contributes only a mild flavour. When you serve these savoury parcels to your guests, the only burning will be in your ears, from the praise you receive, and not the brain-blowing spiciness which is often mistakenly associated with chillies. Courgettes with Tomatoes, Methi and Cumin (see page 130) may be served with the fish parcels.

SERVES 4
PREPARATION TIME: 20–25 MINUTES, PLUS 2–4 HOURS'
MARINATING
COOKING TIME: 8–10 MINUTES

300ml (10fl oz) plain yogurt
280g (10oz) onions, finely chopped
4 garlic cloves, finely chopped
1 teaspoon ground cumin
1 teaspoon ground coriander
1 teaspoon salt
4 x 170g (6oz) portions of cod fillet
4 green chillies
12 sprigs of fresh coriander leaves

◆ Pour the yogurt into a dish large enough to hold the cod fillets. Mix in the onions, garlic, cumin, ground coriander and salt. Add the cod fillets and turn them in the yogurt mixture so that they are evenly coated. Cover and set aside to marinate in the refrigerator for 2–4 hours.

◆ Preheat the oven to 200°C/400°F/Gas 6. Cut 4 sheets of greaseproof paper, each large enough to completely enclose a portion of cod fillet. Remove the cod from the marinade and place one on each sheet of paper.

♦ Divide the marinade between the pieces of fish, spooning it over carefully, and place a whole chilli on top of each. Place 3 sprigs of coriander on top of each piece of fish.

♦ Fold the greaseproof paper over the fish and fold the join in the paper to enclose the fish in a neat parcel. The parcels should resemble Cornish pasties in shape. Place the parcels on a baking tray or roasting tin.

♦ Bake the fish parcels for 8–10 minutes. Transfer the parcels to serving plates. Use a pair of scissors to cut a cross shape to open the top of each parcel and fold the points of the cross back as flaps to expose the fish. Serve immediately.

Chilli-fried Prawns

You really do need plump and juicy prawns for this recipe, which comes from Goa. I have also come across the prawns in Bombay and have always enjoyed them. Fresh prawns are ideal; however, since they are rarely available, use frozen uncooked tiger or king prawns. The spicy prawns make a delicious starter when served on crisp grilled poppadoms, with a dash each of Mint Raita (see page 172) and Clove and Cardamom Dressing (see page 176).

SERVES 4
PREPARATION TIME: 20 MINUTES
COOKING TIME: ABOUT 15 MINUTES

4 tablespoons olive oil or vegetable oil
1 onion, finely chopped
4 garlic cloves, finely chopped
2 green chillies, sliced into rings
2.5cm (1in) fresh root ginger, peeled and grated
$^1/_2$ teaspoon turmeric
$^1/_2$ teaspoon chilli powder
$^1/_2$ teaspoon ground cumin
$^1/_2$ teaspoon ground coriander
20 uncooked tiger prawns, thawed if frozen, shelled
2 tomatoes, quartered, seeded and diced
2 tablespoons coconut milk
$^1/_2$ teaspoon salt
$^1/_2$ tablespoon chopped fresh coriander leaves
2 tablespoons grated fresh coconut or desiccated coconut

♦ Heat the oil in a frying pan. Add the onion and fry until golden brown. Add the garlic, chilli rings and ginger, and fry for 2 minutes, stirring continuously. Stir in the turmeric, chilli powder, cumin and ground coriander.

♦ Reduce the heat to low, then add the prawns and fry for 3 minutes. Stir in the tomatoes, coconut milk and salt, and cook for a further 5 minutes.

♦ Add the coriander, sprinkle with coconut and serve.

Prawns with Coconut Milk

Being English, I attracted significant interest for winning the National Curry Chef of the Year competition and Radio 4's food programme invited me to cook a dish on the show. This superb prawn dish was the ideal choice as it could be made within the short time allowed and because it is relatively easy to prepare the dish is always a winner. The prawns make a great starter or they can be served as a main course. I like to serve spiced basmati rice (page 000) as an accompaniment, with Goan Bread Rolls (see page 162) to mop up the sauce.

SERVES 4
PREPARATION TIME: 20 MINUTES
COOKING TIME: ABOUT 15 MINUTES

2.5cm (1in) fresh root ginger, peeled and grated
3 garlic cloves, finely chopped
1 tablespoon paprika
1 tablespoon ground coriander
1 teaspoon ground cumin
1/4 teaspoon chilli powder
16 tiger prawns, peeled
300ml (10fl oz) coconut milk
1 tablespoon tamarind pulp (see page 12)
1 teaspoon salt
10 fresh curry leaves
1 tablespoon chopped fresh coriander leaves

♦ Pour the 300ml (10fl oz) water into a saucepan. Add the ginger, garlic, paprika, ground coriander, cumin and chilli powder. Bring to the boil and boil until the sauce has reduced by a third.

♦ Reduce the heat, add the prawns and cook gently for 3 minutes. Then pour in the coconut milk and stir in the tamarind pulp and salt. Increase the heat to a medium setting and cook for a further 5 minutes.

♦ Add the curry leaves and remove the pan from the heat. Sprinkle with fresh coriander and serve freshly cooked.

Prawn and Banana Pakora

Chefs are rarely lost for invitations to social gatherings and this is particularly true in India, where people love to entertain. For example, I met a charming family on one flight out to Bombay and they invited me to join them at the wedding they were attending. We stayed in the same hotel in Juhu and met on the evening of the wedding to share a taxi to the Royal Sports Club of India. When we arrived, I quickly realised that I had never been to such a lavish affair before – there were 4000 guests celebrating the marriage of the son of one of India's leading film directors. As the only non-Asian guest, people assumed that I was a film star and I was only too happy to spend the evening signing autographs!

The food was, of course, fantastic, and it was served by dashing waiters wearing white gloves. These pakoras stood out among the myriad of dishes. They were made of fish, but after some experimenting I opted for prawns, which I prefer. They can be served as canapés or as a light snack with chutneys and dips, or as a starter with Mint Raita (see page 172) and Indian Mixed Salad (see page 140).

MAKES 20
PREPARATION TIME: 30 MINUTES
COOKING TIME: ABOUT 3 MINUTES PER BATCH

225g (8oz) self-raising flour
$^1/_2$ teaspoon chilli powder
$^1/_2$ teaspoon turmeric
$^1/_2$ teaspoon garam masala (see page 8)
$^1/_2$ teaspoon salt
2 medium bananas
20 tiger prawns, peeled and thawed if frozen
1 tablespoon chopped fresh coriander leaves
vegetable oil for deep-frying

◆ Sift the flour into a mixing bowl. Then add the chilli powder, turmeric, garam masala and salt.
◆ Gradually mix in 240ml (8fl oz) water, stirring well to make a

thick batter. When all the water is added, beat the batter to ensure that it is smooth.

♦ Lightly crush the bananas with the back of a knife and slice the prawns into 5mm ($^{1}/_{4}$in) pieces. Then add both to the batter and then mix well. Finally, thoroughly mix in the chopped coriander.

♦ Heat the oil for deep frying to 160°C/325°F or until a cube of day-old bread browns in 30–60 seconds. Cook the pakoras in batches, adding the mixture a spoonful at a time. Fry the pakoras for about 3 minutes, until they are puffed and golden, then drain them on kitchen paper. Serve freshly cooked.

Bombay Coriander Mussels

This recipe is inspired by a mussel dish served at one of my favourite restaurants in Bombay. One lunchtime, I walked the crowded pavements of Bombay in search of a restaurant advertising air-conditioning (*sheetal*) until I was thoroughly frazzled and eventually found this place specializing in superb fresh fish, including mussels prepared in the same way as moules à la marinière, but lightly spiced. After the walk, this wonderfully tasty and refreshing dish put the world to rights. I have cut down on the spices and used a creamier coconut milk than the one they used in the restaurant; also I like to add a little fresh coriander right at the end of cooking. Serve Goan Bread Rolls (see page 162) to mop up the delicious cooking liquid.

SERVES 4
PREPARATION TIME: 20 MINUTES
COOKING TIME: ABOUT 10 MINUTES

1kg (2¼lb) mussels, scrubbed and beards removed
1 tablespoon vegetable oil
30g (1oz) butter
55g (2oz) onion, finely chopped
2 large garlic cloves, finely chopped
20 curry leaves
½ teaspoon turmeric
2 teaspoons finely chopped chilli
150ml (5fl oz) white wine
150ml (5fl oz) double cream
150ml (5fl oz) coconut milk
1 teaspoon salt
1 tablespoon chopped fresh coriander leaves

◆ Check the mussels for any open shells. Tap any open mussels sharply and they should close; if the shells do not close, then discard them as the shellfish are dead and should not be eaten.
◆ Heat the oil and butter in a saucepan over high heat. Add the onion, garlic, curry leaves, turmeric and chilli; stir well and

cook for 2 minutes.

♦ Pour in the white wine and heat, without boiling, for 2 minutes, then add the cream and coconut milk. Heat for a further 2 minutes.

♦ Add the mussels, stir well and cover the pan. Cook for 3–5 minutes, until the mussels have opened. Discard any mussels that have not opened.

♦ Finally, add salt to taste and the chopped coriander leaves. Ladle the mussels and soup into bowls and serve immediately.

Vegetables

❖❖

Indian Mashed Potatoes

In India, mashed potatoes are flavoured with chilli, onion, garlic, and chopped fresh coriander leaves. The spicy potato mixture is often rolled into little balls, dipped in a chick pea batter and then deep-fried until golden to make potato bonda. Potato bondas are found in most street restaurants as they are popular aromatic and filling snacks. I have kept this recipe simple and, as such, it makes a great accompaniment for any rich curry.

SERVES 6
PREPARATION TIME: 15 MINUTES
COOKING TIME: 20–30 MINUTES

900g (2lb) potatoes, peeled and cut into large chunks
2 tablespoons vegetable oil
1 teaspoon brown mustard seeds
10 curry leaves
1 onion, finely chopped
2 garlic cloves, finely chopped
2 green chillies, seeded and finely chopped
30g (1oz) butter
90ml (3fl oz) milk
1 teaspoon salt
$^1/_2$ teaspoon garam masala (see page 8)
10 twists of black pepper
1 tablespoon chopped fresh coriander leaves

♦ Cook the potatoes in boiling salted water for 15–20 minutes, or until tender. Drain well.

♦ Meanwhile, heat the oil in a small frying pan over high heat. Add the mustard seeds and curry leaves – they should splutter and spit – and cook for 3 seconds. Reduce the heat to low and add the onion, garlic and chillies. Cook for 5 minutes, or until the onion is translucent.

♦ Mash the potatoes until smooth. You can do this in a blender. Beat in the butter, milk, salt, garam masala and black pepper. Add the onion mixture, mix, and add the coriander.

Roast Potatoes with Ginger, Garlic and Cardamom

Grafton Manor was founded before the Norman Conquest, in the eleventh century. The present manor was commissioned in 1567 by the then Earl of Shrewsbury. Being in such traditional surroundings means that it is impossible not to offer some old favourites on the menu. These potatoes are not too different from the vegetables that have been sown and served through the ages. I have spiced them quite considerably and they are delicious served with any roast poultry or game bird. I like being able to blend the exotic of India with the heritage of the manor house.

SERVES 4
PREPARATION TIME: 10 MINUTES
COOKING TIME: 25–30 MINUTES

4 large Wilja potatoes, quartered
55g (2oz) butter, melted
4 tablespoons vegetable oil
pinch of finely grated fresh root ginger
6 green cardamoms, lightly crushed
2 garlic cloves, finely chopped
salt and black pepper

♦ Preheat the oven to 200°C/400°F/Gas 6. Place the potatoes in a roasting tin. Mix the butter, oil, ginger, cardamoms and garlic. Pour this mixture over the potatoes and season them with salt and pepper.

♦ Roast the potatoes for 25–30 minutes, or until they are golden brown and tender. Shake the tin and turn the potatoes so that they cook evenly. Serve immediately.

Pao Bhaji

Pao bhaji is a great beach dish: the bhaji is cooked in a large, slightly concave wok-type pan and stirred with a metal scraper until it reaches the right consistency. The bhaji is usually served on small metal plates with small bread rolls known as pao. If you eat this in India, always ask for it to be served hot as many tourists suffer stomach upsets as a result of eating beach food that has not been properly cooked. Serve with Goan Bread Rolls (see page 162) as a snack, or as an accompaniment to any Indian main dish.

SERVES 4
PREPARATION TIME: 10 MINUTES
COOKING TIME: ABOUT 30 MINUTES

675g (1$^{1}/_{2}$lb) potatoes
5 tablespoons ghee
1 teaspoon brown mustard seeds
10 curry leaves
1 large green chilli, seeded and finely diced
225g (8oz) tomatoes, roughly chopped
1 onion, finely chopped
1 teaspoon garam masala (see page 8)
$^{3}/_{4}$ teaspoon salt
1 tablespoon chopped fresh coriander leaves
juice of 1 lime

- Boil the potatoes in salted water for about 20 minutes, or until tender. Drain and cut into 5mm ($^{1}/_{4}$in) dice.
- Heat the ghee in a frying pan. Add the brown mustard seeds, curry leaves and chilli. Stir well and cook for 30 seconds, then add the potatoes and tomatoes. Stir again before adding the onion.
- Cook, stirring often, until the potatoes and tomatoes have broken up. Mix in the garam masala and salt until thoroughly combined.
- Finish by adding the chopped fresh coriander leaves and lime juice at the last minute. Serve immediately.

Spinach and Black Pepper Potatoes

Potatoes and spinach always go together well but the dish, often known as saag aloo, can be disappointing, with the spinach over-cooked to a dull and unappealing grey colour – the opposite of the desired result. I fry the potatoes until they are golden, infusing them with turmeric and cracked black pepper, then add the spinach at the last moment so that it remains fresh. When prepared like this, the dish is colourful and served at its best. Crack the peppercorns in a mortar, using a pestle.

SERVES 4
PREPARATION TIME: 10 MINUTES
COOKING TIME: ABOUT 25 MINUTES

6 tablespoons ghee
$^1/_2$ teaspoon brown mustard seeds
1 teaspoon black peppercorns, cracked
$^1/_2$ teaspoon turmeric
675g (1$^1/_2$lb) potatoes, cut into even wedges
115g (4oz) spinach, stalks removed and washed
$^1/_2$ teaspoon salt

- ◆ Heat the ghee in a frying pan. Add the mustard seeds and black pepper, then add the turmeric and stir well.
- ◆ Add the potatoes and fry for 5 minutes, stirring occasionally, until they are a golden yellow. Reduce the heat and continue to cook until the potatoes are soft.
- ◆ Add the spinach and allow it to wilt over the potatoes for a few seconds before stirring it in. Add the salt and cook until the spinach has all wilted and is just cooked. Serve immediately.

Cauliflower and Potato Curry

My father, an ambitious and talented person, who moved to Grafton Manor as a child in 1945 with his parents, eventually came up with the great idea of being self-sufficient. So he bought ducks, geese, sheep and pigs, and grew vegetables. With the very seasonal British climate, growing vegetables means that you often find yourself with a great glut and this recipe is ideal for using up a surplus of potatoes and cauliflower.

SERVES 4
PREPARATION TIME: 15 MINUTES
COOKING TIME: 20–30 MINUTES

4 tablespoons vegetable oil
225g (8oz) onions, finely chopped
3 garlic cloves, finely chopped
2.5cm (1in) fresh root ginger, peeled and grated
$^1/_4$ teaspoon paprika
2 teaspoons ground coriander
$^1/_4$ teaspoon turmeric
3 dried red chillies
2 teaspoons cumin seeds, roasted (see page 12)
120ml (4fl oz) coconut milk
225g (8oz) potatoes, cut into 1cm ($^1/_2$in) dice
225g (8oz) cauliflower, cut into small florets
1 teaspoon salt

◆ Heat the oil in a saucepan. Add the onions and cook them, stirring occasionally, until they are golden brown. Stir in the garlic and ginger, and cook for 2 minutes.

◆ Mix in the paprika, coriander, turmeric, chillies and cumin. Pour in 450ml (15fl oz) water and the coconut milk. Bring to the boil and cook for 3–5 minutes.

◆ Cool slightly, then process until smooth in a blender. Return the sauce to the pan and add the potatoes. Simmer for 8–10 minutes.

◆ Add the cauliflower and salt, cover and simmer for 8–10 minutes, or until the cauliflower is tender. Serve immediately.

Cauliflower and Asafoetida Purée

Cauliflower, one of my favourite vegetables, is a versatile ingredient in Indian cookery. On its own or combined with meat, it can be used in a variety of curries. In this purée, asafoetida contributes its savoury quality to the distinctive flavour of cauliflower.

SERVES 4–6
PREPARATION TIME: 20 MINUTES
COOKING TIME: 6–8 MINUTES

900g (2lb) cauliflower, cut into florets
2 tablespoons vegetable oil
1 onion, finely chopped
3 garlic cloves, finely chopped
$1/4$ teaspoon asafoetida
$1/2$ teaspoon turmeric
150ml (5fl oz) whipping cream
55g (2oz) butter
1 teaspoon salt
10 twists of black pepper
1 teaspoon brown mustard seeds
1 tablespoon chopped fresh coriander leaves

◆ Boil the cauliflower for 3–4 minutes, or until just tender, and drain well.
◆ Heat the vegetable oil in a frying pan. Add the onion, garlic, asafoetida and turmeric, and cook gently for 2–3 minutes, or until the onion is tender. Remove from the heat.
◆ Purée the cauliflower, onion mixture, whipping cream, butter, salt and black pepper in a blender until smooth and then pass the purée through a fine sieve.
◆ Fry the brown mustard seeds in a dry frying pan over medium heat for 30 seconds, until they begin to spit. Add the seeds to the cauliflower purée with the chopped fresh coriander leaves and mix well. Serve immediately.

Mixed Indian Vegetables with Coconut and Coriander

This is a typical vegetable dish from southern India, where it would be served with naan bread as a complete meal. There are certainly more than enough flavours here to satisfy even the most discerning palate and the topping of coconut with chopped fresh coriander leaves adds the final coup-de-grâce.

SERVES 6
PREPARATION TIME: 15 MINUTES
COOKING TIME: ABOUT 15 MINUTES

3 tablespoons mustard oil or vegetable oil
1 tablespoon brown mustard seeds
1 small green chilli, seeded and chopped
$^1/_2$ teaspoon asafoetida
15 curry leaves
225g (8oz) cauliflower, cut into florets
115g (4oz) carrots, cut into 1cm ($^1/_2$in) dice
115g (4oz) small new potatoes
$^1/_2$ teaspoon sugar
1 teaspoon salt
115g (4oz) spinach
1 tablespoon desiccated coconut
1 tablespoon chopped fresh coriander leaves

♦ Heat the oil in a frying pan. Add the mustard seeds, chilli, asafoetida and curry leaves, and stir well.
♦ Reduce the heat to low and add the cauliflower, carrots, potatoes and 120ml (4fl oz) water. Cover and cook for about 10 minutes or until the potatoes are tender.
♦ Stir in the sugar and salt, then add the spinach and cover the pan. Cook for about 1 minute, until the spinach has wilted, then stir well to mix in the spinach.
♦ Sprinkle the chopped fresh coriander leaves and coconut over the top, and serve immediately.

Yellow Pea and Mint Purée

Despite the fact that this dish is yellow, I often think of it as an Indian version of mushy peas. The infusion of the mint is delicious in this yellow pea purée, which is particularly good with any lamb dish.

SERVES 4
PREPARATION TIME: 20 MINUTES, PLUS 2–4 HOURS'
SOAKING
COOKING TIME: ABOUT 1 HOUR

170g (6oz) yellow peas split
2 tablespoons vegetable oil
225g (8oz) onions, finely chopped
2 garlic cloves, finely chopped
8 twists of black pepper
1½ tablespoons chopped fresh mint
1 teaspoon cumin seeds, roasted (see page 12)
salt

♦ Place the peas in a bowl, cover with water and set aside to soak for 2–4 hours.
♦ Heat the oil in a saucepan, then add the onions and garlic. Stir well and cook for 2–3 minutes.
♦ Drain the peas and add them to the onion and garlic. Stir in 600ml (1 pint) water and bring to the boil. Reduce the heat and cover the pan, then simmer for 1 hour.
♦ Stir in the pepper, chopped mint, roasted cumin seeds and salt to taste. Serve immediately.

Pea, Mushroom and Tomato Curry

As a child I loathed mushrooms, but I have now worked them back into my repertoire. They are a wonderful ingredient and their distinctive flavour and texture can add style to a dish. This curry is a great little side dish, but it can also be served as a vegetarian main course. I particularly love the combination of peas and mushrooms with the mild spices. In India, the peas would be added earlier in the cooking process, but I like to add them at the last minute to prevent them from turning grey.

SERVES 6
PREPARATION TIME: 15 MINUTES
COOKING TIME: ABOUT 25 MINUTES

2 tablespoons tomato purée
6 tablespoons vegetable oil
3 garlic cloves, finely chopped
2.5cm (1in) fresh root ginger, peeled and grated
10 curry leaves
1 teaspoon finely chopped green chilli
120ml (4fl oz) whipping cream
1 teaspoon garam masala (see page 8)
115g (4oz) small button mushrooms
115g (4oz) frozen peas, thawed
$^3/_4$ teaspoon salt
1 tablespoon chopped fresh coriander leaves
225g (8oz) onions, sliced

♦ Place the tomato purée and 300ml (10fl oz) water in a saucepan and heat gently for 3 minutes.
♦ Heat 2 tablespoons oil in a frying pan. Add the garlic, ginger, curry leaves and chilli, then fry for 30–60 seconds, stirring well. Remove from the heat and add to the tomato liquid.
♦ Stir in the cream and garam masala, and cook over medium heat, without boiling, for another 3 minutes.

- ♦ Heat 2 tablespoons oil in the frying pan and fry the button mushrooms until browned – this should take 2–3 minutes over high heat. Add to the tomato sauce with the peas, salt and chopped fresh coriander leaves. Reduce the heat to low and simmer gently for 3 minutes.
- ♦ Heat the remaining oil in the frying pan and fry the onions until well browned. Drain on kitchen paper and sprinkle with salt.
- ♦ Pour the pea, mushroom and tomato curry into a bowl and sprinkle the onions on top. Serve immediately.

Courgettes with Tomatoes, Methi and Cumin

I came across this recipe in a restaurant by Anjuna beach in Goa. The fabulous beach, white as snow and lapped by the soft waters of the ocean, is an idyllic place to relax away from the frenzied pace of Indian life. A row of little beach restaurants forms a backdrop to the sand and palm trees, and they serve delicious food – perfect after a day in the sun. Trade was brisk on Wednesdays. The restaurants were packed, oozing with the vitality that makes India so distinctive – that spiritual ease mingling awkwardly with a tremendous passion for ceaseless activity.

After exploring the beach, I chose a restaurant and, deciding to eat something vegetarian, ordered courgettes. The restaurant was busy and the hard-working waiters seemed to have ten arms each. When my courgettes finally arrived in an earthenware dish, with chutney and bread rolls, they were exquisitely prepared. This is delicious with Red Snapper with Tamarind (see page 108).

SERVES 6
PREPARATION TIME: 30 MINUTES
COOKING TIME: 10–15 MINUTES

450g (1lb) courgettes
4 tablespoons olive oil
1 small onion, finely chopped
4 garlic cloves, finely chopped
1 teaspoon cumin seeds, roasted (see page 12)
2.5cm (1in) fresh root ginger, peeled and grated
1 teaspoon turmeric
1 teaspoon chilli powder
1 teaspoon dried methi leaves
1 teaspoon salt
10 twists of black pepper
225g (8oz) can plum tomatoes, drained
55g (2oz) frozen peas
1 tablespoon chopped fresh coriander leaves

- ◆ Top and tail the courgettes, then cut them into 5mm ($^1\!/\!4$in) cubes.
- ◆ Heat the olive oil in a saucepan. Add the onion and cook for about 3 minutes, until it softens. Stir in the garlic, cumin seeds, ginger and courgettes, and cook for 5 minutes. Stir in the turmeric, chilli powder, dried fenugreek, salt and pepper.
- ◆ Coarsely chop the tomatoes and add them to the courgettes. Reduce the heat to low and simmer for 3 minutes.
- ◆ Add the peas and chopped coriander. Stir well for a few seconds until the peas are hot and serve.

Cabbage with Peas, Cumin and Baby Turnips

This simple, tasty vegetable dish is ideal as a light supper dish or it makes an excellent accompaniment for roast chicken or beef. When baby turnips are not available, use larger vegetables and cut them into 2.5cm (1in) cubes: they taste just as good even though they do not look as attractive.

SERVES 4
PREPARATION TIME: 15 MINUTES
COOKING TIME: 6 MINUTES

4 tablespoons vegetable oil
1 teaspoon cumin seeds, roasted
1 savoy cabbage, shredded
12 baby turnips, cooked
115g (4oz) frozen peas
$^{1}/_{2}$ teaspoon salt
10 twists of black pepper
$^{1}/_{2}$ teaspoon garam masala (see page 8)
1 tablespoon chopped fresh coriander leaves

♦ Heat the vegetable oil in a saucepan over high heat. Add the cumin seeds and cook for 10 seconds.
♦ Stir in the cabbage, reduce the heat to medium and add the turnips. Stir in the peas, salt, pepper and garam masala, and cook for 5 minutes.
♦ Sprinkle with the chopped fresh coriander leaves and serve immediately.

Spicy Tomatoes with Brown Mustard Seeds

I first tasted this dish in a very expensive restaurant in central Bombay where I took some friends for lunch. From its rather modest exterior, the restaurant looked cheap, but the marble floors and walls inside gave the appearance of a palace. The marble was also cooling in the midday heat. Preferring a light lunch, I opted for chicken kebab with spicy tomatoes and when they arrived, they were carried by a smartly dressed waiter in traditional Indian costume. Although cooked to perfection, the usual tandoori tikka kebab paled into insignificance compared to the fabulous tomatoes. They were flavoured with mustard and fennel seeds, and finished with coriander. I was so impressed that I asked for the recipe. I have used canned tomatoes in this version. The dish can be served hot or cold, and is an important part of the Smoked Salmon and Chick Pea Noodle Salad (see page 26). The tomatoes can also be served as a vegetable side dish with any Indian main course, but is especially good with Tandoori Lamb's Liver (see page 100).

SERVES 6
PREPARATION TIME: 5 MINUTES
COOKING TIME: 30 MINUTES

3 tablespoons vegetable oil
1 onion, finely chopped
6 garlic cloves, finely chopped
$^1/_2$ teaspoon chilli powder
1 teaspoon turmeric
1 teaspoon brown mustard seeds
1 teaspoon fennel seeds
340g (12oz) can peeled plum tomatoes
$^1/_2$ teaspoon salt
$^1/_2$ teaspoon ground coriander

♦ Heat the oil in a saucepan. Add the onion and garlic, stir in well for 1 minute and then reduce the heat to low. Cook until the onions and garlic have browned slightly, stirring occasionally.

♦ Add the chilli powder and turmeric, mix well and then stir in the mustard seeds and fennel seeds.

♦ Pour in the tomatoes and break them up with a spoon until they are lightly mashed. Simmer gently for 20 minutes, or until the mixture has reduced to a thick consistency.

♦ Add the salt and ground coriander, stir well and serve immediately.

Roasted Cumin Couscous

I have never visited North Africa, but a friend returned from there totally obsessed by all things Moroccan. So I prepared some traditional couscous with one of my favourite curries in an effort to silence him on the subject. For me, couscous conjures up images of crowded bazaars, carpet-salesmen and aged men hunched over glasses of green tea in smoky Moroccan cafes, but I also wanted to serve it with curries. The result surprised us both and the meal was so delicious that my friend never mentioned Morocco again; instead he became preoccupied with the idea of visiting India!

This blend of culinary cultures is special – the flavour and texture of couscous go particularly well with rich curries and it makes an interesting change from rice or dhal.

SERVES 4–6
PREPARATION TIME: 10 MINUTES
COOKING TIME: 35–45 MINUTES

225g (8oz) couscous
1 teaspoon cumin seeds, roasted
150ml (5fl oz) Chicken Stock (see page 170)
3 tablespoons vegetable oil
340g (12oz) onions, sliced
1 tablespoon chopped fresh coriander
salt

◆ Place the cous cous in a bowl and add the roasted cumin and salt to taste.
◆ Bring the chicken stock to the boil, then immediately pour it over the couscous and stir well. Cover and set aside for 20–25 minutes, stirring occasionally.
◆ Heat the vegetable oil in a frying pan over high heat and add the onions. Cook for 5 minutes, stirring continuously. Reduce the heat and cook for a further 10 minutes, or until the onions are golden brown.
◆ Mix the onions into the couscous with salt to taste. Add the chopped fresh coriander leaves and serve immediately.

Salads

⬥⬥
⬥

Tomato, Onion and Coriander Salad

This salad is similar to those served in Indian restaurants, but its preparation is far superior. Try and get tomatoes that are just ripe, but slightly sharp – if possible, use tomatoes sold on the vine. I find the salad refreshing with grilled meats and kebabs, and it is an ideal, easy-to-prepare accompaniment for barbecued foods.

SERVES 4–6
PREPARATION TIME: 15 MINUTES

7 ripe tomatoes, thinly sliced
55g (2oz) onion, finely chopped
good pinch of salt
pinch of sugar
10 twists of black pepper
2 teaspoons olive oil
1 tablespoon chopped fresh coriander leaves
$^1/_2$ teaspoon ground roasted cumin (see page 12)

◆ Arrange the tomato slices overlapping on a large round plate: start at the outside and work around towards the middle.
◆ Sprinkle the onion, salt and sugar over the tomatoes. Then grind the twists of the pepper over the tomatoes.
◆ Trickle the olive oil over the salad. Finish with chopped fresh coriander leaves and roasted cumin.

White Radish, Mint and Horseradish Salad

White radishes are far milder and slightly more moist than the little red radishes that are traditional in British salads. I first sampled this salad at a friend's house in Bombay. I have added horseradish and olive oil, both delicious ingredients in their own right and the perfect complements for white radishes. This salad is good with any Indian meal.

SERVES 4

PREPARATION TIME: 10 MINUTES

340g (12oz) white radish, peeled and finely sliced
55g (2oz) onion, finely chopped
$^1/_2$ green chilli, seeded and finely chopped
1 tablespoon chopped fresh coriander leaves
1 tablespoon chopped fresh mint
1 teaspoon sugar
$^1/_2$ teaspoon Sambar Powder (see page 000), optional
$^1/_4$ teaspoon salt
3 tablespoons olive oil
2 teaspoons creamed horseradish

♦ Use a 30cm (12in) plate if possible. Starting from the centre, fan the white radish slices so that they cover the whole plate.
♦ Sprinkle the radish slices evenly with onion, green chilli, chopped fresh coriander leaves, mint, sugar, sambar powder and salt.
♦ Mix the olive oil and horseradish, and then pour this dressing over the white radish.

Indian Mixed Salad

This is very easy to prepare, but the freshest of ingredients are essential. In India, the severe heat means that salad ingredients wilt if they are left out and if you buy them from a road-side stall they can also be a little dusty as the traffic sprays stalls liberally with dust. At its best, this salad is an ideal antidote to the heat of the day. I like to serve it with a large pot of mint raita, which really brings out the flavours to the full. Frozen peas can be used: simply add them to boiling water, bring back to the boil and drain, then refresh under cold water to prevent further cooking.

SERVES 4
PREPARATION TIME: 20 MINUTES
COOKING TIME: 3 MINUTES

115g (4oz) green beans
115g (4oz) onion, finely chopped
115g (4oz) tomatoes, seeded and cut into 5mm ($^{1}/_{4}$in) dice
115g (4oz) cucumber, cut into 5mm ($^{1}/_{4}$in) dice
115g (4oz) frozen peas, cooked
$^{1}/_{2}$ teaspoon salt
1 tablespoon chopped fresh coriander leaves

♦ Top and tail the green beans and cut them into 2.5cm (1in) lengths. Cook the beans in boiling water for 3 minutes. Drain and refresh under cold water, then drain thoroughly and set aside.

♦ Place the chopped onion, tomatoes, cucumber and peas in the bowl and mix well. Add the green beans, salt and chopped fresh coriander leaves.

♦ Mix the salad well and serve with a drizzle of Orange and Coriander Dressing (page 175).

Chick pea and Couscous Salad

Grainy couscous and chunky chick peas are terrific together: I adore the combination of the textures and flavours. I have used canned chick peas, but dried ones may be used instead. Soak dried chick peas overnight, then cook them in boiling unsalted water for about 30 minutes, or until they are tender. Drain and rinse under cold water, then drain them again. I serve this salad as part of a grand buffet supper, but it is equally tasty as a light snack, topped with a drizzle of Mint Raita (see page 172).

SERVES 4

PREPARATION TIME: 15 MINUTES, PLUS 25–30 MINUTES' STANDING

115g (4oz) couscous
90ml (3fl oz) boiling Chicken Stock (see page 170) or water
115g (4oz) drained canned chick peas
55g (2oz) cucumber, diced
55g (2oz) onion, finely chopped
1 teaspoon salt
1 tablespoon chopped fresh mint

- ◆ Put the couscous in a bowl and pour the boiling stock or water over it. Mix well, then leave to stand for 25–30 minutes, stirring occasionally. The couscous will become light and fluffy as it absorbs the liquid.
- ◆ Mix the chick peas with the couscous and add the chopped cucumber, onion, salt and mint.

Beetroot, Tomato and Green Chilli Salad

I first sampled this simple, yet effective, salad as a canapé at a house in Bombay. Beetroot, tomato and cucumber were all evenly sliced and cut into circles no larger than 6–7.5cm (2^1/$_2$–3in) in diameter. They were stacked on top of each other, seasoned and sprinkled with green chilli and coriander. The simple concoction was so delicious that, for me, it had more impact than the meal which followed. This salad is a successful accompaniment for any Indian food, but I like serving it with chicken dishes, as the tender vegetables go particularly well with succulent chicken.

SERVES 4
PREPARATION TIME: 10 MINUTES, PLUS 2 HOURS' CHILLING

4 medium tomatoes, quartered and seeded
115g (4oz) cucumber, cut into 5mm (^{1}/$_4$in) dice
1 onion, finely chopped
1 green chilli, seeded and finely chopped
^{1}/$_2$ teaspoon salt
1 tablespoon chopped fresh coriander leaves
170g (6oz) beetroot, cooked and cut into 5mm (^{1}/$_4$in) dice

♦ Cut the tomato quarters in half and place in a bowl with the cucumber, onion and green chilli.
♦ Add the salt and chopped fresh coriander leaves and mix well. Cover and place in the refrigerator for 2 hours or until the salad is well chilled.
♦ Add the beetroot, stir well and serve immediately.

Rice & Dhal

❖❖
❖

Spiced Basmati Rice

I am not a great rice eater, but I do have a weakness for this recipe. I love the slightly sticky texture and the fragrant combination of the basmati rice with spices. In most Indian households rice is served plain boiled as an accompaniment to fish curry or a chicken dish; I have tasted some excellent, and unusual, rice dishes in restaurants, especially Biryanis. This rice can be served as an accompaniment for most Indian dishes; it is also especially good for Biryanis.

SERVES 4–6
PREPARATION TIME: 5 MINUTES
COOKING TIME: ABOUT 15 MINUTES

2 tablespoons vegetable oil
2 tablespoons finely chopped onion
1 teaspoon finely chopped garlic
10 curry leaves
225g (8oz) basmati rice
1$^{1}/_{2}$ teaspoons rice masala mix (available in Asian supermarkets)
1$^{1}/_{2}$ teaspoons salt
1 teaspoon chopped fresh coriander leaves

◆ Heat the vegetable oil in a saucepan. Add the onion, garlic and curry leaves to the hot oil, then reduce the heat and cook gently for 1 minute.
◆ Add the rice and the rice masala mix. Stir well until the rice is coated in the oil, then pour in the water.
◆ Add the salt and bring to the boil, then reduce the heat to the lowest setting and cover the pan. Simmer for 10–12 minutes, or until the rice is cooked and tender.
◆ Stir the rice – which should be slightly sticky – then add the chopped coriander and serve immediately.

Fragrant Sweetcorn Rice

Sweetcorn is one of the most succulent and delicious vegetables. One of the local farmers used to grow a field of corn for cattle feed and around the edges of the field there were always a few plants that were raided by local children or hikers. There is nothing like freshly picked corn, char-grilled, rolled in butter, seasoned with black pepper and a little sea salt – it is just utterly delicious. In this recipe, canned or frozen sweetcorn adds a certain zest to the rice, but if you happen to live next to a field of corn, the fresh vegetable will do just as well! This is especially good with Goan Pork Pies (see page 36).

SERVES 4–6
PREPARATION TIME: 5 MINUTES
COOKING TIME: ABOUT 15 MINUTES

2 tablespoons vegetable oil
55g (2oz) onion, finely chopped
3 garlic cloves, finely chopped
115g (4oz) drained canned or frozen sweetcorn
225g (8oz) basmati rice
pinch of ground cardamom
$^3/_4$ teaspoon salt
1 tablespoon chopped fresh coriander leaves

♦ Heat the oil in a saucepan. Add the onion, stir well and cook over medium heat until the onion is soft.
♦ Stir in the garlic and sweetcorn, then add the rice and cook for 30 seconds. Add the ground cardamom and salt.
♦ Pour in 600ml (1 pint) water, bring to the boil and reduce the heat to the lowest setting. Cover and cook gently for 8–10 minutes, or until the rice is cooked.
♦ Add the chopped coriander and serve immediately.

Tomato and Coriander Rice

Rice dishes are good when properly cooked, but it is easy to end up with a result that is too dry, starchy or congealed. This recipe completely dispels the view held by some people that rice must always be plain. Here the fragrant rice is cooked with puréed tomatoes and infused with coriander to give a result that is similar to a rich risotto. The rice can be served with almost any Indian meal, but I think it goes particularly well with Colonial Turkey Curry (see page 72) or Hyderabadi Eggs (see page 40).

SERVES 4
PREPARATION TIME: 15 MINUTES, PLUS 30 MINUTES'
SOAKING
COOKING TIME: 10–15 MINUTES

225g (8oz) basmati rice
400g (14oz) tomatoes, quartered
3 garlic cloves, finely chopped
2 tablespoons vegetable oil
3 tablespoons finely chopped onion
1 teaspoon coriander seeds
6 green cardamoms
1 teaspoon ground coriander
1 teaspoon salt
1 tablespoon chopped fresh coriander leaves

♦ Soak the rice in cold water to cover for 30 minutes. Drain.
♦ Purée the tomatoes in a blender and measure the pulp: you need 450ml (15fl oz). Return the measured pulp to the blender and add the garlic, then blend again until smooth.
♦ Heat the oil in a saucepan over high heat. Add the onion and coriander seeds. Stir well and cook for 2 minutes.
♦ Reduce the heat to low and then add the rice, cardamoms and ground coriander. Pour in the tomato pulp and 120ml (4fl oz) water. Bring to the boil, cover and simmer for 8–10 minutes or until the rice is just cooked.
♦ Add the salt and fresh coriander. Serve immediately.

Buttered Almond and Raisin Rice

In this recipe, cooked rice is dressed with melted butter and then baked. A north Indian flavour is provided by adding almonds and raisins. I like to serve the baked rice with Chicken with Black Pepper and Cardamom (see page 59).

SERVES 4

PREPARATION TIME: 5 MINUTES, PLUS 30 MINUTES'
SOAKING

COOKING TIME: 45 MINUTES

225g (8oz) long-grain rice
55g (2oz) raisins
30g (1oz) flaked almonds
$^{3}/_{4}$ teaspoon salt
10 twists of black pepper
55g (2oz) ghee

♦ Soak the rice in water for 30 minutes. Drain the rice and boil it in plenty of lightly salted water for about 10 minutes, until the grains are tender but slightly undercooked, with a slight starchy bite.

♦ Preheat the oven to 150°C/300°F/Gas 2. Drain and rinse under cold water, then turn it into an ovenproof dish or casserole. Add the raisins.

♦ Toast the almonds under the grill until they turn golden brown, turning them often to prevent them from burning. Add the almonds to the rice with the salt and pepper and mix well.

♦ Melt the ghee and pour it evenly over the rice. Cover and bake for 30 minutes. Serve immediately.

Basmati Rice with Smoked Oysters

The idea for this dish first occurred to me one Hogmanay. As I was busy celebrating the New Year, it struck me that my culinary repertoire was devoid of any hint of Scottish food. So Scotland's finest oysters found their way into India's most famous rice in a delicious contemporary rice dish and I have served it with Indian roast turkey ever since, regardless of the season. I am fortunate enough to have my own smoker, so I buy the freshest of oysters and then lightly smoke them myself. If you cannot buy good-quality fresh smoked oysters, then canned oysters can be used instead.

SERVES 4–6
PREPARATION TIME: 5 MINUTES
COOKING TIME: ABOUT 15 MINUTES

3 tablespoons vegetable oil
1 garlic clove, finely chopped
1 onion, finely chopped
225g (8oz) basmati rice
2 teaspoons salt
8 smoked oysters
1 tablespoon chopped fresh coriander leaves

- ◆ Heat the oil in a saucepan. Add the garlic and onion, and cook until the onion is soft.
- ◆ Stir in the rice and cook for 30 seconds. Add the salt and oysters, then pour in 600ml (1 pint) water and bring to the boil.
- ◆ Reduce the heat to low, cover and cook for 8–10 minutes, or until the rice is tender.
- ◆ Finally, add the chopped coriander and serve immediately.

Goan Risotto

Goa is the place to experience the most spectacular sunsets, preferably with a cool Kingfisher beer in one of the many beach restaurants, watching the fishermen preparing their boats for the next morning and local families packing away after a long day on the beach. Goan risotto is popular with the local fishermen and it is a truly multicultural feast, with chorizo sausage, black olives and chillies alongside curry leaves, cinnamon and cloves. I have used Arborio rice in this recipe, which I prefer for its wonderfully sticky texture when cooked, but you can also use basmati rice. Serve Goan Bread Rolls (see page 162) and/or Indian Salsa (see page 177) with the risotto.

SERVES 4–6
PREPARATION TIME: 10 MINUTES
COOKING TIME: ABOUT 25 MINUTES

5 tablespoons olive oil
10 pieces cinnamon bark or 5cm (2in) cinnamon stick
6 cloves
10 black peppercorns
20 curry leaves
1 medium green chilli, seeded and sliced
1 onion, sliced
3 garlic cloves, coarsely chopped
5cm (2in) fresh root ginger, peeled and coarsely chopped
225g (8oz) arborio rice
115g (4oz) chorizo sausage, sliced
10 black olives, pitted
600ml (1 pint) Chicken Stock (see page 70)
55g (2oz) frozen peas
1 tablespoon chopped fresh coriander leaves
1 teaspoon salt

♦ Heat the olive oil in a saucepan over high heat. Add the cinnamon, cloves and black peppercorns; these should sizzle. Then add the curry leaves and sliced chilli, and stir well for 1–2 minutes.

- ◆ Add the onion, reduce the heat to medium and continue to cook, stirring, until the onions brown slightly.
- ◆ Meanwhile, place the garlic and ginger in a blender. Pour in 240ml (8fl oz) water and process the mixture to a smooth paste.
- ◆ Reduce the heat to low and add the rice to the pan, stirring it with the onion. Then pour in the garlic and ginger paste and again stir well.
- ◆ Add the chorizo sausage and black olives. Stir in the chicken stock and bring to the boil. Reduce the heat to low, cover the pan and cook for 15 minutes, or until the rice is cooked.
- ◆ Add the peas, chopped coriander and salt. Stir well to heat the peas through and serve immediately.

Gujarati Red Dhal

The vast majority of Gujaratis are vegetarian, so dhal is an important part of their diet. This is one of their most loved dishes; toor dhal and red lentils are cooked slowly and infused with browned onions and asafoetida. Even those non-Asians who are dubious about dhal are usually impressed by this true classic.

SERVES 6
PREPARATION TIME: 5 MINUTES
COOKING TIME: ABOUT 40 MINUTES

6 tablespoons vegetable oil
115g (4oz) red lentils
115g (4oz) toor dhal
1 onion, sliced
1 teaspoon asafoetida
1 teaspoon cumin seeds, roasted (see page 12)
salt

◆ Heat 4 tablespoons oil in a small saucepan. Add the red lentils and toor dhal, and stir well for 30 seconds.

◆ Pour in 600ml (1 pint) water and add salt to taste, reduce the heat to low and cook the dhal very gently for about 25–30 minutes, or until tender. Do make sure that there is still a little bite left in the toor dhal at the end of cooking as they should not be allowed to lose their shape.

◆ Heat the remaining oil in a frying pan. Add the onion and fry it until it is red-brown. Add the asafoetida, mix well, then add it to the dhal with the roasted cumin. Serve immediately.

Brigadier's Butter Dhal

Travelling in India demands patience as you are likely to spend long periods waiting for things to happen, without really understanding why. My tactic is to copy the Indian people, who simply shrug, blame delay on the heavens and find somewhere cool to sit. Believe me, they find nothing more comical than the sight of an agitated Westerner demanding to know why the train, plane or ferry is late. In India this is the equivalent of walking into a British post office and demanding to know why no-one ever sends you letters.

On a flight to Goa, as a delay crept towards six hours, I chatted to a fellow traveller and by the time we boarded the aeroplane we were as close as old friends. His brother was a Brigadier in the Indian army and stationed at Goa. We swapped telephone numbers and he invited me to meet his brother. A day later, my new friend called and we arranged a meeting. The brigadier was charming and he showed me around his house, the gardens and mango plantation, then entertained me to a vegetarian lunch of dhals and chapatis. One particular bright red dhal was outstanding and I was so enthusiastic about it, that I finished the whole bowl without realising it. My hospitable host was not remotely offended by my lapse in manners; on the contrary, he sent me on my way with a little party-pack, consisting of more dhal and, most importantly, the recipe!

SERVES 6

PREPARATION TIME: 10 MINUTES, PLUS OVERNIGHT SOAKING

COOKING TIME: 1 HOUR

225g (8oz) red kidney beans, soaked overnight
225g (8oz) mung beans
225g (8oz) red lentils
1 teaspoon turmeric
1 tablespoon ghee
1 teaspoon asafoetida
1 onion, halved and sliced

1 teaspoon cumin seeds, roasted (see page 12)
1 teaspoon salt
225g (8oz) butter
3 tablespoons chopped fresh coriander leaves

♦ Place the red kidney beans, mung beans and red lentils in a saucepan and pour in 1.75 litres (3 pints) water or enough to cover them. Add the turmeric and bring to the boil, reduce the heat, cover and simmer for about 40 minutes, or until tender.

♦ Melt the ghee in a frying pan over medium heat and add the asafoetida, which should sizzle. Then add the onion and fry it until it is golden brown.

♦ Add the onion to the dhal with the roasted cumin seeds and mix well.

♦ Stir in the salt and gently work in the butter. When the butter is completely mixed in, add the chopped coriander and serve.

Chick Pea and Lentil Curry

Chick peas and lentils marry very well in this dish, which has a lovely rich, earthy taste, a pleasing texture and a wonderful flavour of bay leaves. The flavour matures if the curry is made a day (or two) in advance, kept chilled and thoroughly reheated before serving. This is an excellent accompaniment for Venison Rogan Josh (see page 79).

SERVES 4 -6

PREPARATION TIME: 15 MINUTES, PLUS OVERNIGHT SOAKING

COOKING TIME: 35–40 MINUTES

2 tablespoons vegetable oil
1 onion, finely chopped
4 garlic cloves, finely chopped
5cm (2in) fresh root ginger, peeled and grated
4 green cardamoms
$^{1}/_{2}$ teaspoon black peppercorns
4 cloves
3 pieces cinnamon bark
2 bay leaves
115g (4oz) chick peas, soaked overnight and drained
280g (10oz) red lentils
1 teaspoon salt
1 tablespoon finely chopped fresh coriander leaves

- Heat the oil in a saucepan. Add the onion, garlic and ginger, and cook gently for 2–3 minutes, until the onion is translucent and softened.
- Add the cardamoms, black peppercorns, cloves, cinnamon bark and bay leaves and fry for a further 2 minutes.
- Stir in the soaked chick peas and red lentils, then add 1.2 litres (2 pints) water. Bring to the boil, reduce the heat and simmer for 30 minutes or until the chick peas and lentils are cooked. The chick peas should be tender.
- Just before serving add the salt and coriander and mix well.

Chick Pea Ratatouille

Chefs learn to pay as little attention as possible to all the delicacies which are constantly being prepared. Even so, at the end of a day of constant rushing and cooking, when it is finally our turn to eat we like to savour the food. After a busy night's service, I sit down with the team of chefs around the kitchen table, open a bottle of wine and we enjoy our supper. This meal can consist of anything from a roast to an Indian meal, but one of our perennial favourites is ratatouille. I thought it would be nice to bring a taste of India to this dish by adding spices and chick peas, and the result is a mild and aromatic dish. It is a splendid accompaniment for all Indian food or it is equally good with a classic roast, or a plain grilled steak.

SERVES 4
PREPARATION TIME: 20 MINUTES, PLUS OVERNIGHT
SOAKING
COOKING TIME: 1 HOUR 10 MINUTES

115g (4oz) chick peas, soaked overnight and drained
6 tablespoons olive oil
1 onion, finely chopped
5cm (2in) fresh root ginger, peeled and grated
4 garlic cloves, finely chopped
1 green pepper, seeded and cut into 5mm (^{1}/4in) dice
1 red pepper, seeded and cut into 5mm (^{1}/4in) dice
2 green chillies, seeded and finely chopped
225g (8oz) courgettes, cut into 5mm (^{1}/4in) dice
^{1}/2 teaspoon ground coriander
1 teaspoon garam masala (see page 8)
^{3}/4 teaspoon ground roasted cumin seeds
6 tomatoes, quartered
1 teaspoon salt
1 tablespoon finely chopped fresh coriander leaves
1 tablespoon finely chopped basil

♦ Cook the chick peas in boiling water for about 45 minutes, or until they are tender. Skim off any scum that rises to the top of the water during boiling.

♦ Heat the olive oil in a saucepan and add the onion, then cook until it is golden brown.

♦ Add the ginger, garlic, green and red peppers, chillies and courgettes to the onion. Stir well and cook until light brown in colour; this should take 6–8 minutes.

♦ Stir in the ground coriander, garam masala and ground roasted cumin. Then add the tomatoes and cooked chick peas, stir well and continue cooking for a further 10 minutes.

♦ Add the salt, chopped coriander and basil, mix well and serve.

Dhal Mackni

One of the most well-known dhals of India originates from the sun-scorched Punjab, a region which slopes evenly and graciously down towards the deserts of Rajahstan. Top Indian chefs pride themselves on how well they can make this Punjabi dhal, which combines whole urid dhal and kidney beans and is enriched with lashings of unsalted butter at the end of cooking. I was lucky enough to learn how to prepare this dish under the direction of a very talented chef, Serinda Singh, head chef at the Taj Gateway Hotel in Hyderabad. This dhal is good with Hyderabadi Lamb with Rice and Peas (see page 82).

SERVES 4–6

PREPARATION TIME: 15 MINUTES, PLUS OVERNIGHT
SOAKING

COOKING TIME: $1^1/_2$ HOURS

225g (8oz) whole urid dhal, soaked overnight and drained
115g (4oz) red kidney beans, soaked overnight and drained
1 onion, finely chopped
5cm (2in) fresh root ginger, peeled and grated
6 garlic cloves, finely chopped
1 teaspoon chilli powder
$^1/_4$ teaspoon salt
115g (4oz) unsalted butter, melted
1 tablespoon finely chopped fresh coriander leaves

♦ Place the urid dhal and red kidney beans in a saucepan and add 1.4 litres ($2^1/_2$ pints) water; this should cover the dhal. Add the onion, ginger, garlic and chilli powder.
♦ Bring to the boil, then reduce the heat and simmer for $1^1/_2$ hours. The dhal should be soft and reduced to the consistency of a thick purée. Mash the dhal with the back of a spoon every 15 minutes during cooking to achieve the required consistency.
♦ Mix in the salt, unsalted butter and chopped coriander. Serve hot.

Baked Haricot Bean Curry

My niece and nephew, Lydia and John, give this recipe their seal of approval, in fact it has become one of their favourites, and they love eating it with pork sausages for supper. It is important to ensure that the haricot beans are cooked until they are properly tender. If you have a slow oven in a cooking range, suitable for overnight cooking, then bake the beans in the oven overnight.

SERVES 4

PREPARATION TIME: 15 MINUTES, PLUS OVERNIGHT SOAKING

COOKING TIME: $3^{1}/_{2}$ HOURS

225g (8oz) dried haricot beans, soaked overnight and drained
3 tablespoons tomato purée
2 teaspoons curry powder (see page 7)
1 teaspoon turmeric
115g (4oz) eating apples, peeled, cored and diced
1 teaspoon salt
2 teaspoons caster sugar
55g (2oz) sultanas
1 tablespoon chopped fresh coriander leaves

◆ Drain the beans and cook them in boiling unsalted water for 30 minutes or until tender.
◆ Meanwhile, stir the tomato purée into 120ml (4fl oz) water in a saucepan and bring to the boil over high heat. Then reduce the heat and mix in the curry powder, turmeric, apples, salt and sugar.
◆ Preheat the oven to 150°C/300°C/Gas 2. Drain the beans and turn them into an ovenproof dish or casserole. Add the tomato and curry sauce. Mix well, add the sultanas, then cover and bake for 3 hours, until the flavours have mingled together.
◆ Add the chopped coriander to the beans and serve immediately.

Chick Pea Noodles

These noodles, made from chick pea flour or gram flour, are made in different shapes and sizes; they are known as sev and are sold all over India. Noodle vendors wait on the platforms at railway stations in Bombay, ready to sell to passengers as the trains arrive. They have to be very quick to avoid a trip to the next station where they would be trespassing on another vendor's patch. The vendors range from young children to old men and as the train stops they call out "Sev, Sev". The competition to sell is so intense that it is an instant, and sad, reminder of the desperate fight for survival which confronts many people in India; I always feel awkward when choosing one vendor instead of another.

Noodles are also served as a pre-dinner snack, mixed with savoury chopped tomatoes and coriander. I keep a tub of these snack noodles handy, just in case friends pop over or there's a good night of television ahead. You will need an Indian noodle-maker for this, so make a point of looking out for one when you visit a large Indian supermarket. This makes a large batch, but the noodles will keep for 10–14 days in an airtight container.

SERVES 15
PREPARATION TIME: 20 MINUTES
COOKING TIME: 5 MINUTES (30–40 SECONDS PER BATCH)

340g (12oz) chick pea flour (gram flour)
1 teaspoon chilli powder
$^1/_2$ teaspoon asafoetida
$^1/_2$ teaspoon turmeric
1 teaspoon salt
2 tablespoons olive oil
vegetable oil for deep frying

♦ Sift the chick pea flour into a bowl and mix in the chilli powder, asafoetida, turmeric and salt. Thoroughly mix in the olive oil, then slowly mix in about 175ml (6fl oz) water, using your hand to knead the mixture into a stiff dough.

♦ Lightly oil the noodle-maker. Place the dough in it and screw on the lid.

♦ Heat the oil for deep frying to 190°C/375°F or until a cube of day-old bread browns in 30 seconds. Then push some of the dough through the noodle-maker or potato ricer, and drop the noodles into the hot oil. Stir the noodles in the oil for 30–40 seconds, until they are crisp and golden.

♦ Use a draining spoon to remove the noodles from the oil and drain them thoroughly on kitchen paper.

♦ Repeat the process, cooking the noodles in small batches until all the dough is used.

Breads

⬩⬧
⬧

Goan Bread Rolls

Early mornings in Goa are wonderful – the air smells clean and fresh and the temperature is invigoratingly cool. One morning I set out to search for the elusive Goan bread roll. Cheap sliced white bread dominates in many parts of Goa and, as a visitor, it is difficult to find true Goa. I had a mad idea that I might be able to drive around very slowly until I saw someone eating bread and then interrogate them to discover a baker! I set off on my Enfield (motorbike) and had travelled about a mile up the road when a young man appeared from nowhere and sat, without invitation, on the pillion of my bike as I was held up in heavy traffic. He was going to buy bread and decided to hitch a lift; being in no position to refuse, I asked if he knew where I could get some decent Goan bread rolls. His wife's brother was the baker and he promised to get the recipe, so he took my address. Months later, back in rainy England, I received a very crumpled letter with the promised recipe. It was worth the wait.

MAKES 15 ROLLS
PREPARATION TIME: ABOUT 1 HOUR
COOKING TIME: ABOUT 15 MINUTES

150ml (5fl oz) boiling water
45g (1^{1}/$_{2}$oz) fresh yeast
^{1}/$_{2}$ teaspoon sugar
675g (1^{1}/$_{2}$lb) strong white baking flour
30g (1oz) butter
1^{1}/$_{2}$ teaspoons salt
1^{1}/$_{2}$ teaspoons sugar
1 tablespoon Panch Phoran (see page 10)
1 tablespoon chopped fresh coriander leaves

♦ Add 300ml (10fl oz) cold water to the boiling water in one jug. Mix the yeast with a little of the water, then gradually add the rest of the water and stir in the sugar. Place this yeast mixture in a warm place and leave it until it is fizzy and slightly frothy (5–8 minutes).

◆ Place the flour in a bowl and rub in the butter. Then mix in the salt, sugar, panch phoran and chopped fresh coriander leaves. Make a well in the middle and pour in the yeast liquid. Gradually work the flour into the liquid to make a smooth dough.

◆ Turn the dough out on to a lightly floured work surface and knead it thoroughly for about 10 minutes, until it is smooth and elastic.

◆ Alternatively, a suitable food processor can be used to mix and then knead the flour mixture and liquid. Follow the manufacturer's instructions for breadmaking in the machine.

◆ Return the dough to a greased bowl, cover with cling film and leave in a warm place until the dough has risen to the top of the bowl. This should take around 20 minutes.

◆ Once the dough has risen, knock it back by patting it firmly before removing the cling film. Turn the dough out on to a well-floured surface and cut it into equal 90g (3oz) pieces. Preheat the oven to 200°C/400°F/Gas 6.

◆ Gently knead a piece of dough and roll it into a ball in the palm of your hand. Place on a tray covered with baking parchment.

◆ Gently draw a sharp knife across the top of the roll to score it and then sprinkle the top with plain flour. Shape the other rolls in the same way and leave in a warm place until doubled in size. This should take about 10 minutes.

◆ Bake for 15 minutes, or until the rolls are pale golden brown on top. Transfer the rolls to a wire rack and leave to cool.

Deep Fried Crispy Bread

These light and crispy breads are pooris that are infused with green chilli and coriander. When fried, they turn a brown green colour and they taste great with all Indian food.

MAKES 8
PREPARATION TIME: 35 MINUTES, PLUS 2 HOURS' RESTING
COOKING TIME: ABOUT 5 MINUTES

225g (8oz) plain flour
1 teaspoon baking powder
1 teaspoon salt
3 tablespoons plain yogurt
1 green chilli, seeded and finely chopped
1 tablespoon chopped fresh coriander leaves
vegetable oil for deep frying

◆ Sift the flour into a bowl. Add the baking powder and salt, then stir in the yogurt and chilli to make a smooth dough. You may need to add a little water if the dough is too dry.
◆ Shape the dough into a ball. Place on a plate, cover with cling film and set aside to rest for 2 hours.
◆ Lightly flour the work surface and divide the dough into eight pieces. Roll a portion of dough into a ball and flatten it with your hand to make a small disc, about 12–15cm (5–6in) in diameter. Repeat with the remaining dough.
◆ Heat the oil for deep frying to 180–190°C/350–375°F or until a cube of day-old bread browns in 30 seconds. Fry the breads one at a time for about 10 seconds on each side. When cooked each disc of dough should be puffed up into a ball. Drain on kitchen paper.
◆ Serve immediately with any Indian meat or vegetarian dish.

Chapatis

Chapatis are the main form of bread eaten all over India. These flat discs of unleavened wheat-flour bread are ideal as snacks, for mopping up sauces or for filling and rolling. Traditionally, these are cooked on a tawa, an Indian griddle; a standard griddle may be used or a heavy-based frying pan will do.

MAKES 10
PREPARATION TIME: 30 MINUTES, PLUS 30 MINUTES'
RESTING
COOKING TIME: ABOUT 5 MINUTES

225g (8oz) wholewheat chapati flour or plain wholewheat flour
1 teaspoon salt
1 tablespoon vegetable oil
flour for dusting

◆ Sift the flour into a bowl and mix in the salt. Add the oil and then gradually mix in 120ml (4fl oz) water, stirring at first, then kneading by hand to make a soft dough.
◆ Form the dough into a ball, place in a clean bowl and cover with cling film. Then set aside to rest for 30 minutes.
◆ Divide the dough into 10 pieces. Dust your hands with a little flour to prevent the dough from sticking to them, then roll a piece of dough into a ball. Flatten the ball between the palms of your hands, dust the work surface with flour and roll out the flattened ball into a 12cm (5in) disk.
◆ Roll out the remaining pieces of dough, covering the breads with a clean tea-towel when they are rolled.
◆ Heat a griddle over medium heat until hot. Cook a chapati for about 30 seconds on each side, until mottled brown, slightly dry and lightly cooked.
◆ Using a pair of metal tongs, hold the chapati over a gas flame on a low heat setting until it is puffed up.
◆ Repeat with the remaining circles of dough. Chapatis are best eaten straight away. If you have to keep them hot, brush them with melted butter or ghee, wrap in foil, and keep warm.

Green Chilli and Coriander Chapatis

These chapatis are flavoured with fresh green chilli and coriander.

MAKES 10
PREPARATION TIME: 30 MINUTES, PLUS 30 MINUTES'
RESTING
COOKING TIME: ABOUT 5 MINUTES

225g (8oz) wholewheat chapati flour or plain wholewheat flour
1 teaspoon salt
1 tablespoon vegetable oil
flour for dusting
3 green chillies, seeded and finely chopped
2 tablespoons finely chopped fresh coriander leaves

- ◆ Sift the flour into a bowl and mix in the salt. Add the oil and then gradually mix in 120ml (4fl oz) water, stirring at first, then knead by hand to make a soft dough.
- ◆ Form the dough into a ball, place in a clean bowl and cover with cling film. Then set aside to rest for 30 minutes.
- ◆ Divide the dough into 10 pieces. Dust your hands with a little flour, then roll each piece of dough into a ball. Flatten the balls between the palms of your hands, dust the work surface with flour and roll out into 12cm (5in) disks.
- ◆ Divide the chopped green chilli and chopped coriander among the chapatis. Gently roll the chilli and coriander into the chapatis, keeping them in shape. Cover with a clean tea-towel.
- ◆ Heat a griddle over medium heat. Cook a chapati for about 30 seconds on each side, until mottled brown.
- ◆ Using a pair of metal tongs, hold the chapati over a gas flame on a low heat setting until it is puffed up.
- ◆ Repeat with the remaining circles of dough. Chapatis are best eaten straight away. If you have to keep them hot, brush them with melted butter or ghee, wrap in foil, and keep warm.

Naan Bread

One of the first things I do when I arrive in India is to order a plate of naan breads. The ones that you get in this country simply cannot be compared to those in India, where they are thin, slightly flaky and melt in your mouth. This recipe is from the Hyderabadi Club and can be reproduced successfully in a very hot oven. I think the Indian breads are so good because they are cooked in tandoori ovens that are very old and thick, producing an intense heat that cooks the breads quickly. In Britain, yeast is often added to the dough, making the naan as thick as duvets.

MAKES 20
PREPARATION TIME: 35 MINUTES, PLUS 30 MINUTES'
RESTING
COOKING TIME: ABOUT 3 MINUTES PER BATCH

985g (2lb 3oz) plain white flour
1 teaspoon baking powder
$1^{1}/_{2}$ teaspoons salt
1 teaspoon caster sugar
2 eggs
985ml ($1^{1}/_{2}$ pints) milk
2 tablespoons vegetable oil

♦ Sift the flour into a mixing bowl and mix in the baking powder, salt and sugar. Make a well in the middle, then add the eggs.

♦ Gradually mix the eggs into the flour mixture, slowly adding the milk to make a smooth dough. Add the oil to the dough and knead it gently by hand for 5 minutes or until smooth.

♦ Form the dough into a ball and place in a clean bowl. Cover and leave to rest in a cool place for 30 minutes.

♦ Preheat the oven to 240°C/475°F/Gas 9 or the hottest setting. Lightly grease as many baking trays as you have or will fit in the oven.

♦ Divide the dough into 20 pieces and roll them into small balls. Set the balls of dough aside, covering them with a clean tea-towel to prevent them from drying out.

- Place a ball of dough into the palm of your hand and press it out with the other hand, then flip the dough from one hand to the other until it forms a round disk measuring about 15cm (6in) in diameter. Pull one side of the disc to form a pear-shaped naan. Shape the remaining balls of dough.
- Heat the greased trays in the oven for 5 minutes or until they are very hot. Place the naan on the hot trays and bake for 3 minutes, or until puffed up and mottled brown in colour. Serve immediately.

Sauces,
Dressings &
Chutneys

❖

Chicken Stock

Indian food does not really call for the use of chicken stock. I saw it used as a base for soup, flavoured with a medley of spices; however, when it finally emerged from the bowels of a particularly vast and rusty saucepan, the soup turned out to be cloudy and particularly flavourless. Apart from that unfortunate example, a good chicken stock is worth its weight in gold. Being a chef, I always have a supply of chicken bones from boning whole birds or portions, or there are leftovers from roasting; alternatively use inexpensive drumsticks or wing joints. Always start with cold water and allow the stock to simmer gently as this will give you a crystal clear liquid; after the initial heating, never allow the stock to boil. The stock will keep in a refrigerator for up to 5 days. If you make too much for immediate use, remember that stock freezes very well and it will keep for up to 6 months.

MAKES 1.2 LITRES (2 PINTS)
PREPARATION TIME: 1 HOUR AND 30 MINUTES

3 tablespoons vegetable oil
1.8kg (4lb) chicken bones, drumsticks or wings (or a mixture of wings and drumsticks)
1 onion, cut into 6 pieces
3 carrots, cut into 5cm (2in) pieces
1 leek, chopped
8 garlic cloves

♦ Heat the oil in a large saucepan and add the chicken bones, drumsticks or wings, onion, carrots, leek and garlic. Stir well and cook for 5–10 minutes, stirring every minute or so, until the bones have browned slightly. Do not allow them to burn, or the stock will take on a bitter, burnt flavour.
♦ Add 2 litres (3^1/$_2$ pints) cold water. Do not add hot water or the stock will be cloudy. Bring to the boil and reduce the heat so that the stock simmers gently. Cook for 1 hour.
♦ Remove from the heat and strain through a fine sieve into a bowl. Leave to stand for about 3 minutes, then skim off any fat.

Tomato Butter Sauce

There is no better feeling than selecting ingredients you have grown yourself, and the taste of tomatoes fresh from the vine is one that is very hard to beat. I grow tomatoes, so this is probably why I like using them in my cookery, especially in salads and some sauces. This sauce is one of my favourites: it is very light and buttery, and it is delicious with most dishes, especially grilled meats and kebabs. I think it tastes terrific with char-grilled chicken, as the char-grilled flavour marries wonderfully with the aromatic sauce infused with methi.

Makes 600ml (1 pint)
Preparation time: 35 minutes

900g (2lb) tomatoes, quartered
1 teaspoon dried methi
$1/2$ teaspoon chilli powder
1 teaspoon garam masala (see page 8)
1 tablespoon double cream
1 teaspoon salt
1 tablespoon lemon juice
55g (2oz) butter

◆ Pour 450ml (15fl oz) water into a saucepan and add the tomatoes. Bring to the boil, reduce the heat and simmer gently, stirring occasionally to break up the tomatoes, for 15–20 minutes, or until the tomatoes are broken down.

◆ Sieve the sauce, then return it to the rinsed-out pan. Add the methi, chilli powder and garam masala. Return to a low heat.

◆ Stir in the cream, salt and lemon juice. Finally, add the butter, mixing it in until it melts. Serve immediately.

Mint Raita

Yogurt – or kurd, as it is known in India – is eaten as a digestive to calm the stomach and also to calm any excessive heat from eating something a bit spicy. I have always found that kurd in India is slightly sharper in taste than the yogurt we have in Britain, and it often has a watery residue on the surface. Raita is usually infused with chopped tomatoes and cucumber in India, but rarely with mint, as is often the case in this country. I like both recipes, so here I have combined diced cucumber and mint jelly for a quick, easy and irresistible result.

SERVES 6
PREPARATION TIME: 15 MINUTES

3 tablespoons mint jelly
600ml (1 pint) plain yogurt
1^1/$_2$ teaspoons finely chopped mint
pinch of paprika
1 tablespoon finely diced cucumber

♦ Place the mint jelly in a bowl and microwave for 1 minute to melt. Add to the yogurt along with the chopped mint, paprika and diced cucumber. Mix well and chill.

Coriander Pesto

This is based on the classic Italian pesto, made with pine kernels, garlic and Parmesan cheese, but it has lots of coriander instead of basil. Of course, the Italians use this type of sauce mostly with pasta, but I think that it goes very well with Indian food, adding distinctive flavours to the dishes it accompanies.

MAKES 340G (12OZ)
PREPARATION TIME: 15 MINUTES

225g (8oz) pine nuts
115g (4oz) fresh Parmesan cheese, grated
3 garlic cloves
140g (5oz) fresh coriander leaves
pinch of sea salt
300ml (10fl oz) olive oil

♦ Place the pine nuts, Parmesan cheese, garlic, coriander and sea salt in a blender or food processor. Process for 30 seconds or until the ingredients are thoroughly combined – it does not matter if the ingredients are slightly roughly chopped.
♦ With the motor running, add the olive oil and blend until well mixed.
♦ Place in a sterilized jar or airtight container and store in the refrigerator. This will keep in the refrigerator for up to 1 month.

Spicy Cucumber Yogurt

I find cucumber extremely refreshing and delicious on a hot day. This is a simple recipe, but one which is absolutely ideal for barbecues on summer evenings. This will keep in a refrigerator for up to 3 days. It can be served with Vegetable Pakoras (see page 44) or Lamb and Cashew Nut Kofti (see page 35) as a snack or a starter.

SERVES 4
PREPARATION TIME: 15 MINUTES

240ml (8fl oz) plain yogurt
225g (8oz) cucumber, quartered lengthways and cut into 1cm
($^{1}/_{2}$in) wedges
55g (2oz) onion, finely chopped
2 green chillies, seeded and chopped
1 teaspoon paprika
$^{1}/_{2}$ teaspoon brown mustard seeds
$^{1}/_{2}$ teaspoon salt
pinch of sugar
1 tablespoon chopped fresh coriander leaves

♦ Combine the yogurt, cucumber wedges, onion and green chillies in a bowl. Mix well.
♦ Stir in the paprika, mustard seeds, salt and sugar. Finally stir in the chopped fresh coriander leaves Chill for 1–2 hours before serving.

Orange and Coriander Dressing

I believe that salads benefit enormously from spicy and novel dressings and this one fits the bill perfectly. The zesty orange and fresh coriander work well together and the tart flavours of this dressing really bring out the best in green salads and vegetables. You can coarsely crush coriander seeds on a chopping board using the side of a large knife blade. This dressing will keep in an airtight container in the refrigerator for up to a week. Serve it with Tomato, Onion and Coriander Salad (see page 138) or Indian Mixed Salad (see page 140).

MAKES 360ML (12FL OZ)
PREPARATION TIME: 10 MINUTES

240ml (8fl oz) olive oil
2 tablespoons white wine vinegar
2 tablespoons Dijon mustard
grated rind and juice of 1 orange
pinch of sugar
1 teaspoon sea salt
1 tablespoon coriander seeds, coarsely ground
1 tablespoon chopped fresh coriander leaves

◆ Place the olive oil, white wine vinegar and Dijon mustard in a bowl and whisk together well. Add the orange rind and juice, sugar and sea salt and whisk well again.

◆ To finish, add the coarsely ground coriander seeds and the chopped fresh coriander leaves. Chill before serving.

Clove and Cardamom Dressing

This is an unusual, rich and dark dressing that originates from northern India. It will keep for up to a week in the refrigerator and makes a wonderful dip for pakoras and popadoms. It is especially good with Sambar (see page 11).

MAKES ABOUT 300ML (10FL OZ)
PREPARATION TIME: 20 MINUTES

115g (4oz) brown sugar
1 teaspoon cloves
6 green cardamoms
$^1/_2$ teaspoon chilli powder
1 teaspoon ground ginger
1 teaspoon amchoor powder
1 teaspoon cumin seeds

◆ Pour 240ml (8fl oz) water into a small saucepan and add the brown sugar. Bring to the boil and reduce to a syrup. Remove from the heat.
◆ Process the cloves and cardamoms to a smooth powder in a blender and then add to the syrup. Add the chilli powder, ground ginger and amchoor powder to the syrup and stir well.
◆ Heat a small heavy-based frying pan over high heat. Add the cumin seeds and roast them for 10–15 seconds, shaking the pan well all the time. Add to the syrup and cook for a further 3 minutes. Allow to cool before serving.

Indian Salsa

We often have a modest selection of Indian delicacies such as chicken and sweetcorn cakes, with dhal dumplings, raita and Indian salsa for lunch. This salsa is great for such a meal and it makes a good, quick starter when served with a couple of handfuls of Chick-Pea Noodles (see page 159). Always serve it well chilled.

SERVES 4–6
PREPARATION TIME: 30 MINUTES, PLUS TWO HOURS'
CHILLING
COOKING TIME: 2 MINUTES

8 ripe tomatoes, quartered and seeded
1 teaspoon brown mustard seeds
225g (8oz) red onions, finely chopped
2 medium green chillies, halved, seeded and finely chopped
$^1/_2$ teaspoon salt
1 tablespoon chopped fresh mint
1 tablespoon chopped fresh coriander leaves

◆ Cut the tomatoes into 5mm ($^1/_4$in) dice. Heat a small heavy-based frying pan over high heat and add the brown mustard seeds; they should spit and sizzle, so be careful to stand at a distance. Add the tomatoes and fry very quickly for 20–30 seconds.

◆ Remove the tomatoes from the heat and add the onions, chillies, salt, chopped mint and coriander. Mix well.

◆ Cool the salsa, then chill it for 2 hours before serving.

Dried Apricot Chutney

This chutney will keep for up to a month in an airtight jar in the refrigerator.

MAKES 550G (1¼LB)
PREPARATION TIME: 20 MINUTES, PLUS 4–8 HOURS'
SOAKING
COOKING TIME: 20 MINUTES

280g (10oz) dried apricots
280ml (9½fl oz) white wine vinegar
4 tablespoons peeled and grated fresh root ginger
10 garlic cloves, finely chopped
3 tablespoons ground almonds
280g (10oz) sugar
1 teaspoon salt
2 teaspoons chilli powder
1 teaspoon ground cardamom

♦ Put the apricots in a bowl and pour in enough water to cover them. Cover and leave to soak for 4–8 hours.
♦ In a saucepan, bring the apricots and their soaking water to the boil. Simmer for about 10 minutes.
♦ Cool the apricots slightly, then purée them in a blender.
♦ Heat the vinegar, ginger, garlic, almonds, sugar, salt and chilli powder in a saucepan until the sugar has dissolved and formed a syrup. Stir in the apricot purée and simmer, stirring occasionally, for 10 minutes.
♦ When the apricot mixture has thickened, add the ground cardamom and allow to cool.
♦ Place in sterilized jars or an airtight container.

Note
Use sterilizing fluid (the type used for babies' bottles) available from supermarkets to thoroughly clean jars or containers used for storing chutneys and similar items that will be kept for some time.

Brinjal Pickle

Indian markets have a seductive buzz about them, and the selection of fresh vegetables (all organically grown) is outstanding. After a hard day's work at the Taj Mahal Hotel, I used to arrive at Andheri West Train Station in Bombay at about 9pm and fight my way through the heaving crowds. Thousands of stalls lined the main road to Andheri, and the traders carried on doing business right through until midnight. Walk through any Indian market and you will see row upon row of neatly stacked aubergines. The most popular varieties are the baby vegetables and the large elongated type, which are also fairly common in Britain. I find it impossible to put this pickle away once I have started eating it as I love its richness and find the flavour of the aubergine with the methi (fenugreek) irresistible. The chutney will keep for up to a week in a refrigerator. It can be served with most Indian dishes and is delicious with Goan Bread Rolls (see page 162) .

MAKES 280–340G (10–12OZ) CHUTNEY
PREPARATION TIME: 30 MINUTES
COOKING TIME: 20 MINUTES

225g (8oz) aubergines
3 large green chillies, halved and seeded
4 tablespoons mustard seed oil or olive oil
1 teaspoon ground coriander
$^1/_2$ teaspoon ground mixed spice
$2^1/_2$ tablespoons yellow mustard seeds
1 teaspoon salt
$1^1/_2$ teaspoons dried methi
2 teaspoons prepared English mustard
$2^1/_2$ tablespoons brown sugar
1 tablespoon chopped fresh coriander leaves

◆ Top and tail the aubergines, cut them into quarters lengthways and then cut them across into 5mm ($^1/_4$in) thick slices. Cut the chillies into fine matchstick strips.
◆ Heat the oil in a heavy-based saucepan on a medium heat. Add

the chillies and fry for 20 seconds, then add the sliced aubergines, reduce the heat to low and cook gently, stirring occasionally, for 5 minutes.

♦ Add the ground coriander, mixed spice, mustard seeds, salt, methi, English mustard and brown sugar. Stir well until all ingredients are blended together, then cook gently over low heat until the chutney thickens.

♦ Finally, add the chopped coriander and set the chutney aside to cool. Place in a sterilized jar or airtight container and store in the refrigerator.

Date and Tamarind Chutney

Home-made chutneys are far superior to the ones that you can buy in the shops and they are simple to prepare. This chutney is quite sour and rich, with a wonderful flavour of roasted cumin seeds. This chutney will keep for up to a week in the refrigerator or it can be frozen for up to 3 months.

MAKES 900G (2LB)
PREPARATION TIME: 20 MINUTES
COOKING TIME: 45–60 MINUTES

400g (14oz) tamarind (carved off a sticky block)
400g (14oz) fresh dates, stoned
1 tablespoon amchoor powder
1 teaspoon chilli powder
225g (8oz) brown sugar
1 teaspoon salt

- ◆ Place the tamarind and dates in a saucepan. Pour in 1.2 litres (2 pints) water, then stir in the amchoor powder and chilli powder.
- ◆ Bring to the boil over high heat and then reduce the heat so that the mixture simmers. Cook, stirring every couple of minutes, until the chutney is thick and the dates and tamarind have broken down. This should take 45–60 minutes. If the mixture becomes too thick, add a little water.
- ◆ Stir in the sugar and salt, and then pass the chutney through a sieve into a bowl. Discard the stones and husks that are sieved out. Allow the chutney to cool.
- ◆ Spoon the chutney into sterilized jars or an airtight container and store them in the refrigerator.

Coconut Chutney

This chutney is generally found in southern India and it varies quite widely in spiciness. I have also found variations in texture, with some super-smooth chutneys and others that are coarsely ground, according to taste. This recipe is for a coarse chutney. Desiccated coconut may be used if the fresh type is not available. The chutney should be made and used fresh, but it can be stored for 1–2 days in a covered container in the refrigerator.

MAKES 340G (12OZ)
PREPARATION TIME: 20 MINUTES, PLUS OVERNIGHT
SOAKING

175ml (6fl oz) plain yogurt
2 green chillies, seeded and finely chopped
$^{1}/_{2}$ teaspoon brown mustard seeds
1 teaspoon salt
1 tablespoon chopped fresh coriander leaves
1 tablespoon urid dhal, soaked overnight and drained
115g (4oz) grated fresh coconut or desiccated coconut

◆ Place the yogurt, chillies, mustard seeds, salt and fresh coriander in a blender. Rinse the urid dhal, drain them well and add to the blender.
◆ Process the mixture to a paste, then turn it into a bowl and stir in the coconut.
◆ Transfer to a serving dish and serve freshly made.

Mint Chutney

Mint chutney is often served with tandoori or char-grilled meats; it is also good with pakoras. It is coarsely ground and infused with green chilli, and generally served in small amounts.

PREPARATION TIME: 10 MINUTES

30g (1oz) mint leaves
1 tablespoon finely chopped onion
1 green chilli, seeded and finely chopped
1 teaspoon sugar
1 teaspoon peeled and grated fresh root ginger
1 garlic clove, finely chopped
1 tablespoon lemon juice
large pinch of salt

♦ Place all the ingredients in a blender and process to a coarse paste. Serve immediately or place in a dish, cover and chill. Use the chutney on the day it is prepared.

Tomato Chutney

A few years ago I went through a chutney phase and tried as many different Indian chutneys as I could. This rich, gingery and aromatic chutney beats them all. The secret is to use ripe, sweet tomatoes and infuse them with dried methi. It can be eaten with any Indian food or as a spread for breakfast – if you like a savoury start to the day. It will keep for up to a week in an airtight jar in a refrigerator.

MAKES 900G (2LB)
PREPARATION TIME: 30 MINUTES
COOKING TIME: 15–20 MINUTES

6 tablespoons vegetable oil
225g (8oz) onions, finely chopped
10 garlic cloves, finely chopped
10cm (4in) fresh root ginger, peeled and cut into matchstick strips
8 green cardamoms
1 teaspoon nigella seeds
1 teaspoon dried methi
20 curry leaves
900g (2lb) ripe tomatoes
115g (4oz) caster sugar
$^1/_2$ teaspoon salt

♦ Heat the oil in a saucepan. Add the onions and cook for 3 minutes, stirring them until they brown slightly. Add the garlic, ginger, cardamoms and nigella seeds, stir well and cook for 2 minutes.
♦ Add the methi, curry leaves and tomatoes. Reduce the heat to low and cook gently for 5–10 minutes, allowing the tomatoes to stew. Then break them up with a wooden spoon.
♦ Stir in the sugar and salt, and cook for another 10 minutes, or until the chutney has thickened slightly.
♦ Remove the mixture from the heat and allow to cool. Store in a sterilized jar or airtight container in the refrigerator.

Desserts

❖ ❖
❖

Hyderabadi Apricots

Hyderabad, capital of Andhra Pradesh, is as famous for its food as it is for its pearls and bangles. In India, if you ever mention to someone that you are on your way to Hyderabad, they always lick their lips and look wistful.

I worked for a time in the kitchens of the Taj Gateway Hotel, under the supervision of Serinda Singh, a culinary genius who showed me several of his recipes, including this one. At that time, Tuesday was prohibition day, but tourists were allowed to consume alcohol in their own rooms. So every Tuesday, most of the hotel staff came to my rather cramped quarters for a sundowner! It was during one of these crowded gatherings that Serinda Singh mentioned Hyderabadi apricots and when he discovered that I had never heard of them, he telephoned the kitchen. Ten minutes later, they arrived in a silver bowl and they were fantastic: just apricots with sugar, cardamom and water – simple, but then, the best things usually are. These apricots make a sublime dessert when served with Mango and Coriander Parfait (see page 187).

SERVES 6
PREPARATION TIME: 20 MINUTES,
PLUS OVERNIGHT SOAKING
COOKING TIME: 10 MINUTES

450g (1lb) ready-to-eat dried apricots
115g (4oz) caster sugar
1¹/₂ teaspoons ground cardamom

- ◆ Place the apricots in a bowl and add 450ml (15fl oz) water, then leave to soak overnight.
- ◆ Turn the apricots and their soaking liquid into a saucepan. Add the sugar and ground cardamom. Bring to the boil, reduce the heat and simmer for 10 minutes, or until the apricots are tender.
- ◆ Turn the apricots into a container and leave to cool, then chill them well before serving. Stored in an airtight container in the refrigerator, they will keep for up to 3 weeks.

Mango and Coriander Parfait

Little kulfi (ice cream) stalls lurk everywhere in India, from street corners to ocean side, and men sell it from ice boxes carried on their heads. I have never been brave enough to risk a sample from these vendors as a lot of their produce is home made and hygiene standards can be minimal or non-existent.

This recipe is quite involved and time-consuming, but definitely worth the effort. The pâté à bombe, the culinary term for the syrup-custard base, gives a smooth mixture and prevents it from freezing too hard and bending spoons, something which seems to happen on the hard Indian ice creams so often served. The combination of rich, reduced milk with cardamoms, mango purée and an infusion of fresh coriander leaves is wonderfully refreshing.

MAKES 10
PREPARATION TIME: 1 HOUR, PLUS 24 HOURS FREEZING
COOKING TIME: ABOUT 2–2½ HOURS

4 eggs, separated
225g (8oz) caster sugar
900ml (1½ pints) milk
300ml (10fl oz) whipping cream
5 green cardamoms
200ml (7fl oz) mango purée
1½ teaspoons chopped fresh coriander leaves
pinch of salt

♦ Place a large saucepan of hot water over low heat. Whisk the egg yolks, 100g (3½oz) of the sugar and 75ml (2½fl oz) water together in a heatproof bowl. Stand the bowl over the pan.

♦ Cook for about 1 hour, stirring occasionally, until the mixture is thick and creamy. You should be able to stand the spoon up in the mixture. Remember to check the level of the hot water in the saucepan occasionally and top it up with water from a kettle, if necessary, to keep it just below simmering point. Remove the bowl from the pan and pass the mixture through a fine sieve.

- Meanwhile, combine the milk, cream and cardamoms in a large saucepan and bring to the boil over high heat. Reduce and regulate the heat so that the milk simmers steadily without rising and frothing over.
- Cook until the milk and cream are reduced by three-quarters, to 300ml ($^1/_2$ pint). This will take some time, 1–1$^1/_2$ hours, depending on the size of the pan and how fast the milk simmers. Strain the milk through a fine sieve, then allow it to cool. Stir in the mango purée and chopped coriander.
- Place the egg whites in a clean bowl. Add the salt and a pinch of the remaining sugar, and whisk until the eggs stand in firm peaks. Add the rest of the sugar and continue whisking until the meringue is stiff and glossy.
- Prepare ten individual moulds, about 5cm (2in) both in diameter and in depth. Mix the mango and coriander mixture with the yolk mixture, stirring until smooth and evenly mixed. Then gently fold in the meringue until the mixture is smooth, even and glossy.
- Pour the mixture into the moulds, cover with cling film and place in the freezer. Freeze for 24 hours, until completely firm.
- To serve, hold a very hot damp tea-towel around a mould for a few seconds to loosen the parfait, then invert it on a serving plate and lift off the mould. Repeat with the remaining moulds and serve immediately.

Guava and Lime Sorbet

Guavas are one of the flavours of India and they are on sale everywhere – from the harried hawkers on the streets to the plush food markets that are now being developed. One of the most popular dishes at Grafton Manor is guava duff – fresh guava wrapped in sweet suet pastry and steamed, then served with coconut custard. This sorbet is a delightful infusion of lime and guava and it is stunning served with Rice and Dhal Pudding (see page 198).

SERVES 8
PREPARATION TIME: 30 MINUTES, PLUS CHILLING AND 24 HOURS' FREEZING
COOKING TIME: ABOUT 1 HOUR

1 litre (1³/₄ pints) guava purée
450g (1lb) sugar
grated rind and juice of 1 lime

♦ Put the guava purée in a medium-sized saucepan. Pour in 1 litre (1³/₄ pints) water and add the sugar. Bring to the boil, stirring until the sugar dissolves, then remove from the heat and allow to cool.

♦ Add the lime rind and juice to the purée and chill it in the refrigerator. Chill a suitable freezer container.

♦ Turn the mixture into the container, cover and freeze until a band of frozen mixture has formed around the edge. Chill the bowl and blade of a food processor. Process the part-frozen sorbet in the food processor until smooth, then quickly return it to the freezer.

♦ Leave until the mixture is half frozen, then process it again. Repeat once more, by which time the sorbet should be smooth, thick and free from ice crystals. Return it to the freezer and leave until firm.

Note

Sorbet can be made by hand, but it involves whisking the mixture every 20 minutes during freezing. A sorbetière or ice cream churn is ideal; alternatively, a food processor is completely practical. Turn the freezer to the fast-freeze setting before preparing the mixture: remember to switch the setting back to normal when the sorbet has frozen. The freezing time depends on the freezer, but make the sorbet at least the day before it is required as it will require several hours' freezing.

Follow the manufacturer's instructions for using an ice cream churner or sorbetière.

Mint Kulfi

A combination of crème de menthe and fresh mint produce a fresh-flavoured ice cream that is pleasing on hot summer days.

SERVES 10
PREPARATION TIME: 1 HOUR 10 MINUTES, PLUS FREEZING
FOR 24 HOURS.
COOKING TIME: 2–2$^{1}/_{2}$ HOURS

8 egg yolks
170g (6oz) caster sugar
1.75 litres (3 pints) milk
600ml (1 pint) whipping cream
20 green cardamoms
55g (2oz) granulated sugar
6 tablespoons crème de menthe
1 tablespoon chopped fresh mint

◆ Prepare a saucepan of barely simmering water. Place the egg yolks and caster sugar in a heatproof bowl and whisk well. Add 120ml (4fl oz) water and whisk well again. Stand the bowl over a saucepan of hot water and cook slowly, stirring continuously, until the mixture is thick. You should be able to stand a spoon up in the mixture. This may take up to 1 hour.

◆ Pour the milk, cream and cardamoms into a very large, heavy-based saucepan and bring to the boil over medium heat. Regulate the heat so that the milk does not boil over, then allow it to boil until it has reduced by half. This will take about 45 minutes, or longer, depending on the size of the pan. A larger pan allows space for the milk to boil steadily without flowing over the top and so it evaporates more quickly than in a smaller pan. Stir occasionally to prevent the milk from burning.

◆ Add the granulated sugar and cook, stirring, for 2 minutes.

◆ Strain the milk into a large bowl. Cool slightly. Add the crème de menthe, mint and egg mixture. Whisk in well.

◆ Pour the mixture in a freezer container, cool and then chill. Freeze for 24 hours, until firm.

Iced Mango Sorbet

For me, the mango is the prince of fruits. There is nothing quite like splitting open a fresh, ripe mango and gouging out all that sweet, juicy flesh. I often make mango dishes in attempts at recreating some of the pleasure the fruit gives me in India. If the mango is the prince of fruits, then this is the princess of sorbets. I always keep a reassuring portion handy in the freezer, for when I'm feeling wistful and want to remember all the good things about my Indian sojourns. Notes on making sorbet are given with Guava and Lime Sorbet (see page 189).

SERVES 10
PREPARATION TIME: 20 MINUTES, PLUS CHILLING AND FREEZING
COOKING TIME: 10 MINUTES

900ml (1½ pints) mango purée
225g (8oz) sugar
1 tablespoon chopped fresh coriander leaves

◆ Place the mango purée, 600ml (1 pint) water and sugar in a saucepan. Bring slowly to the boil, stirring occasionally, then reduce the heat and simmer for 3 minutes. Remove from the heat and allow to cool.

◆ Add the chopped fresh coriander leaves and chill the mixture. Chill a suitable freezer container.

◆ Turn the mixture into the container, cover and freeze until a band of frozen mixture has formed around the edge. Chill the bowl and blade for the food processor. Process the part-frozen sorbet in the food processor until smooth, then quickly return it to the freezer.

◆ Leave until the mixture is half frozen, then process it again. Repeat once more, until it is smooth, thick and free from ice crystals. Return it to the freezer and leave until firm.

◆ Follow the manufacturer's instructions for using an ice cream churner or sorbetière.

Hot Peppered Pineapple

This unusual dish is one that I have cooked for years and it always raises eyebrows. I first formed the idea of spicing up pineapple by accident when a friend played a trick on me, adding pepper instead of cinnamon to juicy refreshing pineapple. He waited for my grimace of revulsion when I tasted the fruit, but the pineapple was surprisingly tasty and the pepper made a positive contribution. Here the pineapple is cooked with sweet oranges, sugar, butter and generous amounts of black pepper; it is good with Mango and Coriander Parfait (see page 187).

SERVES 4
PREPARATION TIME: 25 MINUTES
COOKING TIME: 15 MINUTES

1 pineapple
55g (2oz) butter
115g (4oz) brown sugar
grated rind of 1 orange and juice of 2 oranges
2 tablespoons brandy
4 green cardamoms
1 teaspoon ground black pepper

◆ Trim both ends off the pineapple with a sharp knife, then cut off the skin, removing all the spiky little spines. Use an apple corer to cut out the tough core of the pineapple and cut four 5mm (¼in) slices.

◆ Melt the butter in a frying pan over low heat. Add the sugar and stir. Add the orange juice and brandy and bring to the boil.

◆ Add the cardamoms, black pepper and pineapple slices. Reduce the heat and simmer for 5 minutes. Turn the pineapple slices over and cook for 5 minutes. The pineapple should now be tender and the sauce should have reduced to a light syrup. If the sauce is too thin increase the heat to high and boil it until it is reduced and syrupy.

◆ Reduce the heat to low, add the orange rind and cook for a final 3 minutes. Serve immediately.

Gulab Jamun with Coconut Custard

On one occasion passengers at Bombay airport were treated to a grand buffet lunch to compensate for flight delays and Gulab Jamun were served as one of the sweets. These little deep-fried dough balls are flavoured with cardamom and drenched with sweet syrup.

SERVES 6
PREPARATION TIME: 20 MINUTES
PLUS 12–24 HOURS SOAKING
COOKING TIME: ABOUT 20 MINUTES

600ml (1 pint) milk
225g (8oz) plain flour
1 teaspoon ground cardamom
225g (8oz) sugar
1 vanilla pod or 2 drops vanilla essence
6 saffron strands
2 drops rosewater
vegetable oil for deep frying
Coconut Custard (see page 000)

♦ Bring the milk to the boil in a fairly large saucepan and boil steadily until it is reduced to 450ml (15fl oz). Watch the milk to ensure that it does not boil over and stir occasionally to prevent it from burning on the base of the pan.
♦ Stir in the flour and ground cardamom and mix to a soft dough. Remove from the heat and set the dough aside to cool.
♦ Mix the sugar and 600ml (1 pint) water in a fairly large saucepan and bring to the boil. Add the vanilla pod or essence and boil until reduced to a light syrup. Remove from the heat, then stir in the saffron strands and rosewater. Put to one side.
♦ Divide the cooled dough into 12 portions and roll them into balls.
♦ Heat the oil for deep frying to 160°C/325°F or until a cube of

day-old bread browns in 30–60 seconds. Fry the balls of dough until golden brown, turning or rolling them over occasionally so that they cook evenly.

♦ Drain the gulab jamun on kitchen paper and then add them to the syrup as they are cooked. Turn the gulab jamun in the syrup to ensure they are all coated, cover and leave to soak for 12–24 hours.

♦ Serve with the Coconut Custard (see page 203).

Bread and Butter Pudding with Cardamom and Lime Custard

This recipe makes a pudding which is far lighter than any I have eaten in India, where the bread is first fried and then soaked in milk, sugar and eggs. The usual technique is to mash the mixture and sprinkle it with nuts before baking. My version is flavoured with cardamom, pistachio nuts and mixed dried fruit; moistened with eggs, sugar, cream and milk; and cooked in a bain marie to ensure that the result is moist and light. Finally, the top is caramelized with icing sugar. Cardamom and Lime Custard, a classic English custard enlivened with cardamom and fresh lime, goes just perfectly with the pudding.

SERVES 4
PREPARATION TIME: 30 MINUTES, PLUS 2–4 HOURS'
STANDING TIME
COOKING TIME: 40–45 MINUTES

300ml (10fl oz) milk
300ml (10fl oz) double cream
1 vanilla pod, split and seeded, or 2 drops vanilla essence
90g (3oz) caster sugar
6 egg yolks
115g (4oz) butter
225g (8oz) white bread, crusts removed and cut into 5mm (^{1}/4in) thick slices
2^1/2 tablespoons finely chopped pistachio nuts
55g (2oz) mixed dried fruit
1 teaspoon ground cardamom
2 tablespoons icing sugar
Cardamom and Lime Custard (see page 204)

♦ Heat the milk and cream together until boiling. Add the vanilla pod or essence, remove from the heat and allow to cool.

- Place the sugar and egg yolks in a bowl and whisk until pale and frothy. Strain the milk, if necessary, to remove the vanilla pod and pour it over the yolk mixture, whisking well.
- Butter a 30 × 23 × 3.5cm (12 × 9 × 1$^{1}/_{2}$in) baking tin or oven-proof dish.
- Butter the slices of bread evenly on both sides and line the base of the buttered dish or tin with a layer of buttered bread.
- Sprinkle with some of the pistachio nuts, dried fruit and ground cardamom, then pour in about a third of the egg and cream mixture. Continue layering the bread and fruit, adding the custard to moisten each layer, and ending with a layer of buttered bread.
- Pour any remaining custard over the top layer and leave the pudding to stand for 2–4 hours.
- Preheat the oven to 200°C/400°F/Gas 6. Cover the pudding with foil and stand it in a roasting tin. Pour water into the outer tin to come up to just below the rim of the outer tin.
- Bake the pudding for 40–45 minutes, until lightly set, puffed up and lightly browned on top.
- You can use a blow torch for this stage or preheat the grill on the hottest setting. Sift the icing sugar over the pudding. Caramelize the icing sugar with the blow torch or place it under a very hot grill. Take care not to burn the top of the pudding.
- Serve immediately with the Cardamom and Lime Custard.

Rice and Dhal Pudding

Green lentils and long-grain rice were the original ingredients that my friend in Bombay used in her dish, but I prefer red lentils and pudding rice. Using dhal in a sweet recipe probably sounds strange, but it is very more-ish. Try serving a large spoonful of strawberry jam with the pudding.

SERVES 4
PREPARATION TIME: 35 MINUTES
COOKING TIME: 25 MINUTES

450ml (15fl oz) milk
300ml (10fl oz) whipping cream
8 green cardamoms
55g (2oz) red lentils
55g (2oz) pudding rice
115g (4oz) sugar
1 teaspoon rosewater

♦ Bring the milk and cream to the boil over medium heat. Add the cardamoms, lentils and rice, reduce the heat to low and simmer gently for 15–20 minutes, stirring occasionally.
♦ Stir in the sugar and cook for 2 minutes, then stir in the rosewater. Remove from the heat and set the pudding aside to rest for 5 minutes, to allow the rosewater to flavour the rice.
♦ Serve either warm or chilled.

Pink Grapefruit with Roasted Cumin

Pink grapefruit are far less harsh than their yellow cousins – some of those can really make your ears flap if you taste a tart one. Although cumin is best known as an ingredient in savoury dishes, it can also be very effective with sweet ingredients; here it combines with pink grapefruit to give refreshingly interesting results. Always roast the seeds beforehand to bring out their full aromatic and nutty flavour. Serve Ginger Yogurt (see page 000) as an accompaniment.

SERVES 4
PREPARATION TIME: 10 MINUTES

4 pink grapefruit
2 teaspoons salt
4 small pinches sugar
2 teaspoons cumin seeds, roasted (see page 12)
16 twists of black pepper

♦ Peel the grapefruit, discarding all the skin and pith. The best way to do this is to trim off the top and base, then stand the fruit firmly on a board and slice off the skin and pith in wide strips from top to bottom.

♦ Cut each grapefruit into 5 slices and arrange these, overlapping, on four plates. Sprinkle with salt, sugar and roasted cumin seeds, lifting the slices as you do so.

♦ Grind 4 twists of black pepper over each plate and serve drizzled with Ginger Yogurt (page 202).

Chocolate and Cinnamon Crème Brûlée

My second chef William Henderson came up with the idea of adding a hint of Indian spice to crème brûlée, which is one of his favourite sweet dishes. One early spring evening, Will and I were sitting on the front lawn mulling over ideas for the next Christmas menu and easing things along with a rather nice bottle of champagne. We really have to start planning Christmas almost before we have recovered from the hangovers from the last one and several glasses of champagne were essential for getting into the swing of thinking about the party season. Will thought a chocolate crème brûlée would be a nice idea for Christmas; I thought of adding cinnamon and we both decided that this spicy innovation called for another bottle of champagne! This is a recipe to impress your friends with its wonderful texture. I always make this the day before to allow time for the brûlée topping to set.

SERVES 6
PREPARATION TIME: 30 MINUTES, PLUS 18 HOURS' CHILLING
COOKING TIME: ABOUT 1 HOUR

4 egg yolks
90g (3oz) caster sugar
115g (4oz) bitter chocolate
4 teaspoons ground cinnamon
600ml (1 pint) whipping or double cream
6 tablespoons demerara sugar

◆ Preheat the oven to 180°C/350°F/Gas 4. Whisk the egg yolks and caster sugar together until pale and thick.

◆ Melt the chocolate in a bowl over a saucepan of hot water, stirring occasionally. Pour the chocolate into the egg yolk mixture, whisking all the time, preferably with an electric whisk on slow speed.

◆ Add the cinnamon and whisk again. Warm the cream very

slightly, just to take the chill off it. Heating it briefly in the microwave saves pouring it into a saucepan.

♦ Whisking all the time, pour the cream into the other ingredients. Pass the mixture through a sieve and pour it into six ramekin dishes.

♦ Stand the ramekins in a roasting tin and pour in water to come about halfway up the outside of the small dishes.

♦ Bake for 55–60 minutes, or until the chocolate custards are lightly set, when they will still be wobbly in the centre.

♦ Remove from the bain marie or tin of water and cool, then chill for 6 hours.

♦ Preheat the grill on the hottest setting. Sprinkle 1 tablespoon demerara sugar over the top of each crème brûlée. Place the crème brûlées under the grill until the sugar has melted and lightly caramelized. Alternatively, use a blowtorch to caramelize the sugar.

♦ Chill the brûlées for 12 hours before serving.

Ginger Yogurt

This is very easy to make and it can be eaten for breakfast or with any fresh fruit. It will keep for up to a week in the refrigerator.

MAKES 360ML (12FL OZ)
PREPARATION TIME: 10 MINUTES

360ml (12fl oz) plain yogurt
5cm (2in) fresh root ginger, peeled and grated
4 teaspoons caster sugar

♦ Mix the yogurt, ginger and caster sugar in a bowl and whisk well.
♦ Chill well before serving as an accompaniment to desserts, with fresh fruit or on its own.

Coconut Custard

This is a classic English custard made with coconut milk – very simple and delicious.

SERVES 6
PREPARATION TIME: 5 MINUTES
COOKING TIME: ABOUT 20 MINUTES

8 egg yolks
125g (4^1/$_2$oz) sugar
3 drops vanilla essence
300ml (10fl oz) coconut milk
300ml (10fl oz) milk

♦ Prepare a saucepan of barely simmering water. Place egg yolks in a heatproof bowl and add the sugar. Whisk the egg yolks and sugar until they are pale and creamy.
♦ Heat the vanilla essence, coconut milk and the milk together until they boil, then remove from the heat and cool for a few seconds. Pour the hot milk mixture into the egg yolk mixture, stirring all the time.
♦ Stand the bowl over the pan of hot water and cook gently, stirring continuously, until the mixture thinly coats the back of a spoon. Do not allow the water in the saucepan to boil or the custard will overheat and curdle.
♦ Remove the bowl from the saucepan as soon as the custard has thickened slightly as overcooking will cause it to curdle. Stand the bowl of custard in a sink or bowl of cold water to cool it quickly and arrest the cooking process.
♦ Serve immediately.

Cardamom and Lime Custard

This custard infused with cardamon and lime is a great accompaniment to Indian Bread and Butter Pudding (page 196) or serve just with plain bananas.

SERVES 4
PREPARATION TIME: 5 MINUTES
COOKING TIME: ABOUT 20 MINUTES

6 egg yolks
125g (4^1/$_2$oz) sugar
600ml (1 pint) milk
6 green cardamoms, lightly crushed
1 vanilla pod, split and seeded, or 3 drops vanilla essence
grated rind of 1 lime and juice of ^{1}/$_2$ lime
1^1/$_2$ teaspoons chopped fresh coriander leaves

♦ Prepare a saucepan of simmering water. Place the egg yolks in a heatproof bowl. Add the sugar and whisk until the mixture is pale and creamy.

♦ Pour the milk into a saucepan. Add the cardamoms and vanilla, then bring slowly to the boil, allowing time for the flavour of the spices to permeate the milk. Allow to cool slightly before straining the milk on to the egg yolk and sugar mixture. Mix well.

♦ Stand the bowl over the pan of hot water and cook gently, stirring continuously, until the mixture thinly coats the back of a spoon. Do not allow the water in the saucepan to boil or the custard will overheat and curdle.

♦ Remove the bowl from the saucepan as soon as the custard has thickened slightly as overcooking will cause it to curdle. Stand the bowl of custard in a sink or bowl of cold water to cool it quickly and arrest the cooking process.

♦ Cool the custard, stirring occasionally to prevent a skin from forming, until it is just lukewarm. Stir in the lime rind and juice, and the chopped coriander. Serve immediately.

Drinks

❖ ❖
❖

Wine

In India, beer is the main alcoholic drink taken with food and Kingfisher is the main brand, sold in litre bottles. Haywoods 2000 or London pilsner are also popular. In Goa, beer is very popular and comes in two strengths: one light and lager based, the other strong and quite malty.

Wine in India is not of good quality and it often resembles vinegary port. However, most Indians are quite proud of this wine, called Boshca and it is expensive, so if you are offered a glass, grit your teeth and knock it back in one go, but decline a second glass. I have suggested a collection of beers and wines that I offer friends when serving Indian food. However, there are no hard and fast rules, so you can drink what you like with your chosen dishes.

White Wine

The choice is limited to wines with sufficient depth of flavour to stand up to the spices. You should not choose a delicate wine, as the taste will be masked by the food. Although German wines are out of fashion at present, their sweetness and lovely acidity go very well with spicier dishes. Care has to be taken in selecting these wines as many are too delicate. A Spätlese or a good Kabinett would be better than the more popular halb-trocken styles. A good all-round choice would be an Alsace Gewürztraminer. The spicy and aromatic flavour of this wine complements the flavours in the food. It is a touch more expensive than other good German whites, but it is worth every penny. Niersteiner Gutes Domtal is a slightly cheaper German white and its sweet flavour is compatible with chicken dishes.

Another suggestion is an oaked Chardonnay, whether it be from Australia, New Zealand, Chile or France. The toasty flavours of the oak enhance the character of the Chardonnay grape in a wine that marries well with many Indian dishes. The Chardonnay Marborough has a refreshingly peachy taste, and is one of my favourites – it goes particularly well with fish dishes and starters.

If you are looking for a crisper, sharper taste, then you might want to consider a Muscat wine or a Chenin Blanc. Muscat has great freshness and is a wonderful partner for all Indian food, especially prawns and particularly when they are cooked with ingredients like coconut milk and coriander. Chenin Blanc is a another suitable crisp and dry white wine from the fertile vineyards of South Africa.

For those of you who are really pushing the boat out, try Mersault. This is a wonderful wine produced by Louis Latour, but it is expensive and should only be drunk at very special Indian dinner parties. It is, however, exquisite, and is especially good with fish dishes.

Red Wine

With red wine the choice is easier: although there must be sufficient body and depth of flavour to balance the dishes, this is a more common characteristic of red wine. For a really robust wine, you might try Don Darias. This rioja is excellent value, and its strength of character, with an oaky vanilla taste, makes it an ideal companion to dark meat curries. French Claret is sometimes known as the Englishman's wine, simply because we drink it so often. You can spend huge amounts of money on it, but there are some good cheaper vintages and I like to drink these with Venison Rogan Josh and lamb dishes. A cheaper and equally flavoursome wine might be found amid the pinotage wines – this sort of wine is excellent with red meats and game.

A fruitier drink is found in Cabernet Sauvignon. The Cabernet grape has become more and more popular recently, and some of the Chilean wines are particularly fine – try Errazuriz or Santa Rita. A slightly fuller flavour comes with a full-bodied Côtes du Rhône wine, which has a warming taste and a hint of spiciness; both the Cabernet Sauvignon and the Côtes du Rhône are ideal for a tray-top supper of steaming authentic curry and dhal, sitting in front of the fire in winter.

Finally, if you are eating lighter Indian food, you would do well to try Barolo. This is one of Italy's most famous wines. It has a ruby red colour, and drinks particularly well in the summer.

Dessert Wine

There is a vast selection of good and inexpensive dessert wines available. You can have a white Bordeaux from Cadillac or Monbazillac, or a sweet Tokay. My all time favourite dessert wine, though, is the Muscat de Beaumes de Venise from the Rhône. I love its elegant and sweet floral flavour, which makes a marvellous accompaniment to Indian desserts. Always serve this wine well chilled.

Beer

The majority of people do not think of wine when they think of curry – most of us will always think of lager! There is no doubt that an ice cold beer is super with a spicy dish. Some of India's finest lagers are now available in this country, a development I have welcomed with much happiness.

Try the Kingfisher (already recommended) or Cobra, another tasty Indian beer that has a slightly smoother taste than Kingfisher. Finally, you might be able to get hold of Lal Toofan, which is a rice beer from Rajahstan.

Alcohol-free Drinks

The following are typical drinks that may be served as cooling refreshment at any time of day. Tea is the number-one drink all over India. Even in the loudest bars, where the local beer flows free, you will find a group of friends sipping tea and passing the time of day. The tea – rich, strong and extremely sweet – can be purchased for about 1 rupee from any tea stall where it is poured into little glass beakers; I find it quite addictive. In private homes the tea is often served in stainless steel beakers and any welcome guest will be offered this humble refreshment.

Lassi, a chilled yogurt drink, is also important – as widely consumed in India as a cup of tea is in Britain. Cooling and refreshing in the heat, lassi comes in a whole range of flavours and it can be mixed thick or thin.

Rosewater Lassi

I prepare a thinner version, which I find more refreshing and less filling, and I particularly like rosewater lassi. I first sampled lassi in the exotic surroundings of the roof-top restaurant at the Taj Mahal Hotel, Bombay, where I was shadowing the sous chef. We sat down after the lunch rush and Harish produced a huge jug of rosewater lassi. The Indian Navy was on manoeuvres in the bay and we soaked up the view of the Gateway of India and the surrounding port. Even in humble settings, lassi is a wonderful and unusual thirst-quencher, and great at any time of day.

SERVES 4
PREPARATION TIME: 10 MINUTES

4 tablespoons plain yogurt
3 teaspoons sugar (or to taste)
$1^1/_4$ teaspoons rosewater or kewra essence
ice cubes to serve

♦ Place the yogurt, sugar, rosewater or kewra in a blender and add 450ml (15fl oz) water, then process thoroughly.
♦ Place ice cubes in four tall glasses and pour the lassi over. Decorate with rose petals and serve.

Orange, Roasted Cumin and Black Pepper Lassi

Orange and roasted cumin go together very well indeed, providing an unusual and surprising contrast between sweet and spice.

SERVES 6
PREPARATION TIME: 10 MINUTES

2 medium oranges, peeled and cut into small pieces
300ml (10fl oz) natural yogurt
2.5cm (1in) fresh root ginger, peeled and grated
pinch of salt
10 twists of black pepper
$^{1}/_{2}$ teaspoon roasted cumin (see page 12)
ice cubes to serve

♦ Place all the ingredients, except the ice, into a blender. Add
300ml (10fl oz) water and process until smooth and frothy.
♦ Place ice cubes in six tall glasses and pour the lassi over. Serve.

Mango Lassi

Mango lassi is a home-made brew sold on the streets of India. It is thick, sweet and delightfully refreshing. Against the riotous colours of a tropical sunset, with the growing hum of nocturnal insects whistling through the air and the first stars blinking from the darkening sky, there is no better way to start an evening than with a cool glass of mango lassi.

SERVES 6
PREPARATION TIME: 15 MINUTES

225g (8oz) fresh mango
300ml (10fl oz) plain yogurt
3 heaped teaspoons sugar
$^3/_4$ teaspoon chopped fresh coriander leaves
ice cubes to serve

♦ Peel the mango and cut the flesh off the stone in large pieces. Roughly chop the flesh and place it in a blender.
♦ Add the yogurt, sugar and 300ml (10fl oz) water. Process until the mixture is smooth, then add the chopped fresh coriander leaves.
♦ Place ice cubes in six glasses and pour in the lassi. Serve immediately.

Masala Tea

This is the sweet, spiced tea of India. I find it addictive and India is the only place on earth where I would drink sweet tea.

SERVES 6
PREPARATION TIME: 15–20 MINUTES

2 tablespoons Assam or Darjeeling tea leaves
240ml (8fl oz) milk
6 cardamom pods, crushed
2 tablespoons granulated sugar
2.5cm (1in) root ginger, cut into 3 pieces

- Pour 1.2 litres (2 pints) water into a saucepan and add the milk. Bring to the boil over a high heat. Add the cardamoms, sugar and ginger, and boil for 8–10 minutes.
- Add the tea leaves and continue to boil for 5 minutes. Remove from the heat and allow to stand for 3 minutes. Strain into a teapot and serve.

Index

Useful Suppliers

Most large supermarkets offer an excellent range of spices and international ingredients. Alternatively, ethnic supermarkets are found in most large towns or cities, and healthfood or wholefood shops are often a good source of international foods, particularly pulses or dhal. The following are examples of the many companies providing mail order services, supplying herbs, spices and specialist ingredients. Look out for advertisements in food magazines. You may have to purchase a larger quantity than you would ideally like, but remember that spices freeze well: double pack them in freezer bags in airtight containers.

Cool Chile Company
P.O. Box 5702
London W11 2GS
Tel: 0870 9021145

Curry Direct
P.O. Box 109
Bridgnorth WV16 4WE
Tel: 01746 761211
Spices, ingredients and
equipment

Fox's Spices Ltd
Masons Road
Stratford upon Avon
Warwickshire CV37 9NF
Tel: 01789 266420/Fax: 01789
267737

Greencades
5 The Apprentice Shop
Merton Abbey Mills

Watermill Way
South Wimbledon
London SW19 2RD
Tel: 0181 543 0519/Fax: 0181
543 3553
Herbs and spices

Hambleden Herbs
Court Farm
Milverton
Somerset TA4 1NF
Tel: 01823 401205

Raja Brothers
162 Ladypool Road
Sparkbrook
Birmingham B12 8JS
Tel: 0121 772 4958/Fax:0121
753 2102
Personal shoppers only, no
mail order